James Robinson Nichols

Fireside Science

A Series of Popular Scientific Essays Upon Subjects Connected With Every-Day Life

James Robinson Nichols

Fireside Science

A Series of Popular Scientific Essays Upon Subjects Connected With Every-Day Life

ISBN/EAN: 9783744674003

Printed in Europe, USA, Canada, Australia, Japan

Cover: Foto ©Thomas Meinert / pixelio.de

More available books at **www.hansebooks.com**

FIRESIDE SCIENCE.

A SERIES OF

POPULAR SCIENTIFIC ESSAYS UPON SUBJECTS
CONNECTED WITH EVERY-DAY LIFE.

BY

JAMES R. NICHOLS, A. M., M. D.,

AUTHOR OF "CHEMISTRY OF THE FARM AND THE SEA," AND EDITOR OF
"BOSTON JOURNAL OF CHEMISTRY."

NEW YORK:
PUBLISHED BY HURD AND HOUGHTON.
Cambridge: Riverside Press.
1872.

TO

THE FAMILY GROUP

WHO BY MY OWN FIRESIDE HAVE LISTENED TO THE READING OF THESE ESSAYS AS THEY CAME FRESH FROM THE PEN,

I DEDICATE THIS LITTLE VOLUME.

PREFACE.

THE essays contained in this volume relate to the science of home life, and the every-day affairs of individuals and families. It has been the aim of the author to present some of the facts of science in their bearings upon hygiene, the arts, agriculture, etc., in a way to interest and instruct those who gather by the fireside, and those who labor in the workshop and the field. In order not to weary and confuse the minds of readers, the essays have been made as brief as possible. It is certain that the general reader cannot be held to the perusal of scientific treatises, if they abound in extended discussions, or are presented with much minuteness of detail. Science can only be attractive to the busy men and women of our time when its facts and instructions are unincumbered with abstract reasonings and technicalities; and also it is needful, if the popular mind is to be interested, that the facts bear upon some definite point or topic. It will not do to skirmish over a wide field, and attempt to bring under one head a dozen branches of a subject. It is manifestly better to give each special consideration, and endeavor to have the statements clear, brief, and accurate. This is the general plan adopted in the preparation of these essays, and it may be stated that it is no untried experiment. Most of them have appeared in the columns of the "Boston Journal of Chemistry" during the past three or four years, and they have been received with favor by many readers in all sections of the country. The longer essays upon agricultural topics have formed the basis for addresses before State Boards of agriculture, farmers' meetings, etc. They give some of the results of the author's observations and experiments at his farm at Lakeside, in Essex County, Massachusetts, and as evidence is afforded that they have supplied valuable facts and hints to those who have listened to the reading of them, it is possible they may serve a useful purpose in aiding other husbandmen in their important labors.

The essays which have been published in the journal in charge of the author have been thoroughly revised, and some portions have been rewritten; and it is hoped that both these, and others found in the volume, will prove entertaining and instructive to the new class of readers to whom they are now introduced.

BOSTON, *November*, 1871.

CONTENTS.

	PAGE
THE ORIGIN AND NATURE OF SPRINGS	1
CHEMISTRY OF A HEN'S EGG	18
REBREATHED AIR	30
CHEMISTRY OF A CIGAR	36
CHEMISTRY OF A PINT OF KEROSENE	48
THE LOST ARTS	61
THE HUMAN HAIR	73
MICHAEL FARADAY	86
CHEMISTRY OF A LUMP OF SUGAR	90
FARM EXPERIMENTS AT LAKESIDE	101
WHAT SHALL WE USE FOR WATER-PIPES?	135
THE CLOTHING WE WEAR	150
THE RELATIONS OF WATER TO AGRICULTURE	156
THE SKIN AND BATHING	186
DIAMONDS AND DIAMOND CUTTING	193
AMONG THE COAL MINERS	203
CHEMISTRY OF THE HUMAN BODY	215
ABOUT QUICKSILVER	222
EXPERIMENTS WITH AIR FURNACES	228
FARM PENCILLINGS AT LAKESIDE	234
REMINISCENCES OF AN EXPERIMENTER	245
INFECTIOUS GERMS	255
THE FOOD OF PLANTS	262

FIRESIDE SCIENCE.

THE ORIGIN AND NATURE OF SPRINGS.

SPRINGS of water are possible upon our earth only from the fact that its various strata or layers have been upheaved from their original beds by internal or volcanic forces. It is indeed curious, that the sparkling spring or brook which breaks from the hillside and meanders through the meadow, an emblem of purity and peace, is born of the earthquake, and exists only in consequence of the terrible havoc which fire and gases have made of the rocky ribs of mother earth.

The elementary facts of geology are sufficient to make plain to every one the truth, that the crust of the earth is not composed of a homogeneous mass of rock with a thin covering of soil superimposed upon it, but rather, that it is made up of a series of strata lying one over another, these having been formed from the deposition of sedimentary matter at the bottom of oceans and seas in former epochs of the world's history. The layers have solidified from various causes, and become rock of one kind and another, and they all rest upon the great mass of igneous rock which forms the mighty framework of the earth's crust. Now it is apparent that if the various strata of the sedimentary rocks had never been disturbed, but had remained in their original level position just as they were formed, rivers, lakes, and springs could have had no existence. There would have been no hills or mountains or valleys, and the waters upon the earth must have rested in vast holes or excavations upon its surface. The rain would have managed to escape by soaking into the porous strata, and remaining there until, in part, driven off by evaporation from internal or solar heat. It could not have formed definite channels or rivers, as it does now, on the slopes found upon every continent. The porous strata or coatings, consisting of the mould, sand, and gravel, would have received the rain, as has been said, and a part of it would undoubtedly have been removed by the agency of heat; but a large portion would have penetrated downward, until it met with strata wholly impervious, and there it would remain until it acquired sufficient pressure to be forced out in all directions into cavities constituting the seas. What an oozy, damp condition of things must have existed during the carboniferous and oölitic epochs, or before the great rock upheavals occurred!

Let us look for a moment at another point of no

little importance, in the geology of springs and rivers. The various strata of sedimentary rocks are by no means alike in physical or chemical constitution: some of them are hard, refractory, insoluble in water; others are soft, easily disintegrated, or worn by the action of water moving over their surfaces. Upon this difference in the structure or solubility of rocks as now arranged, depends, in a great measure, the formation of crevices and gorges, the sources of springs and rivers. The *débris* formed from aqueous action constitute for the most part the material which makes up soils upon the earth's surface, and hence it is plain to see, that with undisturbed strata, the present arrangement of arable soils could not have existed. It is the solution of the constituents of different rocks in percolating water, which renders a mineral spring possible. Of course none of these could have been found if everything was at a dead level, and the strata were quietly reposing as originally deposited.

The breaking up, tilting, contorting, overturning of these rock layers has been complete; and consequently mountains, hills, valleys, precipices, gorges, and rock fissures have been formed, and from them and through them the springs flow, and among them, often at high altitudes, beautiful lakes repose. The number and the distribution of springs in any section depend not only upon the inclination of the strata but upon the character of the rock which prevails. The arrangement of percolating streams below the earth's surface is of course entirely unseen, but it must be, nevertheless, very wonderful and interesting. The water which flows out of an orifice in a rock or in the soil at a given point, may have fallen as rain upon a surface ten, twenty, or five hundred miles distant, and the subterranean river may have wandered in darkness down the sides of distant mountains through sand, marl, and rock fissures, into the valleys below. From thence, it may have been forced up the sides and over other mountains of less altitude, by the well known law which governs fluid equilibrium, until it reached the surface at a favorable opening, and escaped as an ever gushing spring. The geological formations which prevail in any section govern the conditions under which water flows from the earth, whether it be with eruptive force, or feebly, as do most springs that come under our observation. We must remember that the great bulk of the sedimentary rocks, and all of the unstratified, are wholly impervious to water, and in their upheaved condition, it is only through the breaks and seams which prevail that it can find its way into the great subterraneous sand deposits and cavities which exist in many localities. If the geological conditions are such as to afford insufficient surface drainage, so that a water supply is not afforded, it may be possible to reach the reservoirs in the deep strata below by borings, and these extensive perforations are called artesian wells. They are not always successful, as it is impossible, from geological observations, to determine whether the different strata are favorable or unfavorable. It may be that there exists a porous stratum at a distant point of sufficient area to collect the rain-fall, and that there are seams between the impermeable rocks, so that it can pass along down to a lower level; but it is not certain that it is held in the deep basins where we might expect to find it. Dislocations in the strata are common, and through them the water may leak out and seek a lower stratum, or a natural vent, by which it can rise to the surface at a point lower than the well. Any one who engages in deep borings for water does so at considerable risk, as no geologist or chemist can give him positive assurances of success. In this country we have numerous artesian wells, some of them of great depth. The famous St. Louis well is about 1,900 feet deep, and the force with which the water rises is very great. It is however entirely unsuited to domestic uses, being charged with mineral constituents derived from rocks and minerals over and through which it passes in its course. Offensive gases are often mingled with water coming from deep wells, and the temperature is uniformly high. The gases present are usually carburetted hydrogen, and sometimes sulphuretted hydrogen is evolved freely, giving to the water the smell of stale eggs. The temperature of the water depends in a great measure upon the depth of the boring. The well at St. Louis delivers water at a temperature above 100° F., and the water of most other wells is found above 70° F. In winter such water, if pure, would be delightful for washing purposes, but for drinking it would be vapid and nauseous. It is also without atmospheric air, and would need not only to be cooled but to be aerated to fit it for table use. Altogether we may conclude that the deep springs are not very promising sources from which to obtain potable waters.

It has been remarked that the water from artesian wells is derived from great distances. This was shown in a boring at Tours, France, from which, when the borer was withdrawn, quantities of sand and small snail-shells were ejected, which without doubt found their way there from the mountains of Auvergne, thirty miles distant. Eels and small fish have been found in the water of artesian wells, which shows that there is sometimes direct communication through the strata with distant ponds or superficial accumulations of water. The water which falls upon inland mountains and hills, and passes downwards through pervious strata, often finds vent in the sea, and thus the curious spectacle is afforded of a fresh water spring bubbling up through a mass of salt water. Humboldt mentions such a spring as occurring at the mouth of the Rio Sargartos, off Cape Caloche, four hundred yards from land. The inhabitants of Syracuse obtain excellent fresh water by rowing off in boats into the salt sea, and dipping it up into vessels as it rises to the surface from the orifice below. It is difficult to conceive of anything more paradoxical than this.

. If the mean annual temperature of the air is taken as a standard of comparison, it will be found that a majority of springs are *thermal*, or warm springs, the temperature being above the mean of the air of the locality in which they exist. The earth is a great reservoir of heat, and as a rule the heat increases the deeper we descend, and therefore deep springs uniformly supply warm water; cold springs usually flow from superficial rock or soil coverings among hills, and in the gorges of mountains. The elevated points in which they originate are constantly under the influence of cooling winds, and the shade of rocks and trees prevents the action of the solar rays in elevating the temperature. It is not true that the gradual increase of heat in the earth's crust is 1° F. for every fifty feet of descent, although this statement is persistently made in school-books and popular journals. Some years ago experiments were made in a large number of Prussian mines, and it was found that it varied between 1° F. in 21.3 and in 155.5 feet. Other experiments have been made in mines in this country, Mexico, and South America, which prove that the extremes are still greater. Undoubtedly much of this variation is due to the differing conducting power, or specific heat of the formations through which the excavations were made; still it is clear that there is no uniform rate of increase of temperature throughout the earth's crust. If it were true that the rise equals 1° F. for every fifty feet of descent, at a depth of twenty-five miles every known substance would be in a state of fusion. How intense must be the central heat of our globe! for it is impossible to doubt that these fires exist, notwithstanding the cogent arguments which have been urged against the theory. It is this great central ocean of fire which warms the water of our deep wells, and it is often brought to the surface heated to a point actually above that of boiling water. The Icelandic Geysers afford water heated to 248° F., which is 36° above the boiling point. There are springs in California and also in South America, which supply water heated above 200° F., and a very large number scattered over the surface of the earth, which show a temperature of 175° F.

From these high temperatures we may find springs exhibiting every gradation down to 33° F., or 1° above the freezing point.

It is natural to suppose that the warm water which gushes from the earth in copious supply would be turned to some practical account, and that baths might be constructed in the vicinity of, or over these outlets, or that the water might be used for heating buildings. There are numerous celebrated bathing establishments in Italy, France, Germany, and other countries, where the waters are heated by internal volcanic fires, and many of these thermal springs have been used for bathing purposes from the earliest times. There is a celebrated hot spring at Baiæ, near Naples, much frequented by the ancient Romans, the waters of which are hot enough to cook eggs, and other food substances. We well remember the terrible perspiration into which we were thrown several years ago while attempting to explore the cave in the rock in which this spring is found. The air was like that of an oven, and the blinding, scalding clouds of steam rendered a prolonged stay in the cave impossible. In the province of Auvergne, in France, there is a small town, Eaux Chaudes, in which all the houses are warmed during the winter months, by hot spring-water conducted through them in pipes. There are several towns in our own country which are lighted by the carburetted hydrogen gas which flows spontaneously from the earth; and there is good reason for believing that in these localities water sufficiently warm for heating the dwellings might be readily obtained by boring at no great depth. It is quite reasonable to suppose that there are localities in this and other countries where it is possible to obtain from water and gas springs sufficient material to light and warm buildings, and also sufficient mechanical power to work machinery effectively. The surprising capabilities of mother earth are as yet but imperfectly understood, but in process of time, as our needs increase and more knowledge is obtained of hidden resources, we shall be able to avail ourselves of many salutary agents of which we have not the slightest conception at present.

No class of springs have awakened greater interest, or provoked more discussion, than what are known as *intermitting* springs. Such springs are active or inactive for longer or shorter periods of time, some of them having an intermission in the flow, of several minutes' or hours' duration, while others stop flowing altogether for days. The spring at Poterbrunnen, in Westphalia, ceases for six hours and then flows again for six hours, and the volume of water is such that it turns three mills in its course. Another spring, in the Jura Mountains, intermits every six minutes; and there is still another, in France, which flows for 36½ minutes, and then ceases for 33½ minutes. In England there are several intermitting springs of an interesting character, and in this country there are a considerable number. In Vermont we have visited a spring which intermits as often as every three minutes, but the flow of water is small. The new spouting spring at Saratoga is an intermittent spring of a rather peculiar nature, as the flow does not entirely cease, and the intermissions are not for a fixed period of time. This is obviously due to obstructions in the flow of water, caused by carbonic acid gas. This gas in large quantities accompanies the water, and sometimes it fills the tube and for an instant holds the water back, or permits but a small flow; then the gas is forced out, and the water rises again. Undoubtedly the irregular evolution of gas causes many springs to intermit, but there are also other causes which operate to produce such results. When springs have a connection with the sea through pervious strata, the tide would operate to produce an irregular flow. At flood tide the pressure would cause a flow; at the ebb, the condition of things would be reversed, and it would cease. Some of the spring-bearing strata conduct water after the form or under the conditions of the siphon, and consequently they flow intermittently. The great Geysers in Iceland, to which allusion has been made, are the most remarkable examples of intermittent springs which the world affords. The smallest of these flows for fifteen or twenty minutes every two hours, and the largest only once in twenty-four or thirty hours. Some interesting papers have been written upon these springs, in which ingenious theories have been advanced to account for the phenomena presented. The most reasonable explanation is that vapor or steam holds back the column of water at intervals in the same way as does the gas in other springs, and that it is only when this steam pressure is forced to give way that the water flows, and thus the periodic accumulation of steam in the pipes causes intermittent flow.

The term mineral or medicinal has been given to a class of springs, the waters of which hold in solution considerable quantities of mineral salts or agents which are used medicinally. From the most remote ages invalids have resorted to mineral springs with the view of being relieved of certain maladies, and in this country and other parts of the world there are springs which have acquired a reputation for extraordinary curative properties. The arrangement of mineral springs at Saratoga is certainly wonderful; and we cannot recur to a group in any part of the world which will at all compare with these, in potency of medicinal character, or singular variety of constituents. It is impossible for any one, however unobservant or careless, to visit these springs and not be impressed with the singularity of the display which is afforded, of natural waters holding large quantities of mineral substances in complex combination. Many of the agents contained in the waters are extraordinary and rare, and in studying their composition it has been found difficult to point out a dozen inorganic substances used medicinally, which are not found in the waters of some one or more of the group of springs at Saratoga. Here are iron, iodine, bromine, lithium, magnesia, lime, soda, potassa, sulphur, baryta, strontia, alumina, and a great variety of other agents, held in perfect solution in the waters, conferring upon them a great diversity in appearance and taste, and also a great diversity in medicinal effects. The nature of the strata and rocks through and over which these waters flow, in their course towards the outlets, must be very singular in chemical composition. The sources of many of the springs are probably quite distant, and they bubble up from considerable depths. They are artesian in character, although a majority have come to the surface through natural channels. It is probable that the nature of the underlying strata and rocks is such, at Saratoga, that it would be impossible to make a boring at any point within a radius of half a dozen miles of Congress Spring without striking a water supply holding a large quantity of mineral matter. This interesting section seems to be a point towards which waters of a remarkable character gravitate, and probably the supply will be kept up for ages to come, as it has been in the ages which have elapsed. There is wonderful uniformity in the admixtures of mineral matters with the waters, as the various analyses show. No sensible variation in the amount of inorganic constituents has been discovered during the years since chemical science was sufficiently advanced to enable correct determinations to be made. The admixtures are so complex and so perfect that it is difficult, or in fact quite impossible, to imitate them in the laboratory. Nature, in her chemical combinations and admixtures, surpasses art, and it is not probable that human science, turned in the direction of the fabrication of mineral water, will ever become so perfect in its imitations as to render the pilgrimage of invalids to Nature's fountain at Saratoga unnecessary.

It is a singular fact that there are numerous waters in this country and in Europe, medically in high repute, which are distinguished among chemists only for their *purity*. The celebrated waters of Pfeffers, to which Martin Luther resorted and was cured of terrible hypochondriasis, are almost chemically pure, and so are those of Wildbad and Baden, to which thousands flock from all parts of the world. These fountains, as resorts for invalids, date back to the time of the Roman Conquest, when Cæsar bathed in and drank the waters, extolling their virtues. Several of the springs at Ballston and Saratoga contain so few saline particles that they should be reckoned as nothing in judging of the source of the therapeutic influence of the waters.

At this point the inquiry arises, From whence comes the remedial power of these fountains? By their use, are diseases ameliorated or cured? or are alleged beneficial effects purely imaginary, and without foundation in fact? The latter hypothesis is unsatisfactory, and there is a vast amount of unimpeachable testimony in the way of its ready reception. Indeed, it is not necessary to resort to this method of disposing of the difficulty. In the examination, we find little more than pure water to be the agent employed; and, if remedial benefits result, the pure lymph of the fountain, innocent of salt, should have all the credit. And is not water a medicine? When drank in quantities beyond the demands of thirst, in many diseases, especially those arising from arrested metamorphosis, it produces marked salutary results. I venture the opinion, derived from experience and observation, that simple water, as a therapeutic agent, is not sufficiently well understood among educated medical men. Its employment has been long abused by empirics, and therefore has fallen into discredit. In withdrawing attention from it, an important auxiliary in the treatment of disease is overlooked.

The consideration of its internal use, in connection with the so-called mineral springs, leads to some observations upon that form of employment. It cannot be doubted that morbid accumulations of effete matter in the tissues and alimentary canal are more readily removed by draughts of water, at proper times and in proper quantities, than by any other agent; and here we learn the secret regarding the benefits obtained by invalids at mineral springs. A large majority of those who resort to them are suffering from atonic conditions of the stomach and bowels. Constipation is almost certain to be a prominent trouble, and then follow nervousness, hypochondriasis, and a long train of evils. At home no more than a tumbler of water may be drank in the twenty-four hours; at the springs, three or four are swallowed before breakfast in the morning. The fæcal accumulations of the intestines are softened, peristaltic motions awakened, the food ducts are cleansed, and smiling health returns. The "minerals" and the salts of course get the credit, — *aqua pura* none at all. If the saline or solid constituents of a pint of almost any of the aperient spring-waters are isolated, and taken in a dry state, they seldom produce any action upon the bowels; but if they are redissolved and drank, laxative effects follow. This would seem to prove that a combination of water and salts is needful; but when it is found by further experiment that the water produces intestinal motion without the salts, a new view presents itself.

It is quite evident that the benefits received by invalids at mineral springs cannot be attributed solely to any unusual condition of the waters, but in a great degree to the liquid itself, taken medicinally, or at unusual hours and in unusual quantities. It must, however, be conceded that a change of air, habits, society, etc., has much to do in the work of restoration; and therefore, although the water employed for domestic purposes at home may be equally efficacious, a resort to springs should not be discouraged, especially among those whose pecuniary means are ample. The proofs which science affords that the physical and chemical character of waters famous for their medicinal virtues differs in no essential particular from those in ordinary use in families, certainly favors the view that, having regard to temperature, quantity, and time of employment, the home waters may be used medicinally for the relief of a large class of affections.

CHEMISTRY OF A HEN'S EGG.

IT is presumed that but few of those who break the shells of the cooked eggs of our common domestic fowls, at the breakfast table, ever think of the wonderful nature of the structure they crush, or of the complex chemical nature of the contents consumed as food. To a large majority of people, an egg is an egg, and nothing more. If the multitude were inclined to inquire into the composition of this curious embryotic substance, the impatience of hunger which universally prevails at the commencement of the morning meal would render the hour quite unpropitious, and therefore we hardly expect to secure the reader's attention until the time arrives for lighting the evening lamp.

Before proceeding to inquire into the interior composition of the egg, we will consider the exterior covering, or the shell, the physical and chemical structure of which is exceedingly interesting and wonderful. The white, fragile cortex called the shell, composed of mineral matter, is not the tight, compact covering which it appears to be, for it is everywhere perforated with a multitude of holes, too small to be discerned with the naked eye, but which, with the aid of a microscope, are distinctly revealed. Under the microscope, the shell appears like a sieve, or it more closely resembles the white perforated paper sold by stationers. Through these holes there is constant evaporation going on, so that an egg, from the day that it is dropped by the hen to the moment when it is consumed, is losing weight, and diminishing in volume. This process goes on much more rapidly in hot weather than in cold, and consequently perfect eggs are not so readily procured in summer as in winter. If by any means we stop this evaporative process, the egg remains sound and good for a great length of time. Covering the shell with an impervious varnish, or with mutton suet, or lard, aids greatly in their preservation. The substance used to stop transpiration must not be soluble in watery fluids, or liable to be readily removed. By chemical agencies, that is, by actually filling up the little holes in the shell by lime placed in contact in solution (the solution holding the proper chemical substances to form an impervious coating of carbonate of lime over the entire surface), we have preserved eggs for months and even years in a sweet condition. Not long ago, eggs broken in our laboratory were found to be quite fresh, which, according to the memorandum made upon the vessel, were placed in the solution in May, 1867.

The shell of the egg is lined upon its interior everywhere with a very thin but pretty tough membrane, which, dividing at or very near the obtuse end, forms a little bag which is filled with air. In new-laid eggs, this follicle appears very small, but it becomes larger when the egg is kept. In breaking an egg this membrane is removed with the shell, to which it adheres, and therefore is regarded as a part of it, which it is not.

The shell proper is made up mostly of earthy materials, of which 97 per cent. is carbonate of lime. The remainder is composed of two per cent. of animal matter, and one of phosphate of lime and magnesia. Carbonate of lime is the same material of which our marble quarries and chalk beds are composed; it is lime, or oxide of calcium, combined with carbonic acid, and is a hard, insoluble mineral substance, which does not appear to form any portion of the food of fowls. Now, where does the hen procure this substance with which to form the shell? If we confine fowls in a room, and feed them with any of the cereal grains, excluding all sand, dust, or earthy matter, they will go on for a time and lay eggs, each one having a perfect shell, made up of the same calcareous elements. Vauquelin, the distinguished chemist, shut up a hen ten days, and fed her exclusively upon oats, of which she consumed 7,474 grains in weight. During this time four eggs were laid, the shells of which weighed nearly 409 grains; of this amount 276 grains were carbonate of lime, 17½ phosphate of lime, and 10 gluten. But there is only a little carbonate of lime in oats, and from whence could these 409 grains of the rocky material have been derived? The answer to this question opens up some of the most curious and wonderful facts connected with animal chemistry, and affords glimpses of many of the operations of organic life, which, to the common mind, seem in the highest degree paradoxical and perplexing. The body of a bird, like that of a man, is but a piece of chemical apparatus, made capable of transforming hard and fixed substances into others of a very unlike nature. In oats there is contained phosphate of lime, with an abundance of silica, and the stomach and assimilating organs of the birds are made capable of decomposing or rending asunder the lime salt, and forming with the silica a silicate of lime. This new body is itself made to undergo decomposition, and the base is combined with carbonic acid, forming carbonate of lime. The carbonic acid is probably derived from the atmosphere, or more directly perhaps from the blood. These chemical changes among hard inorganic bodies are certainly wonderful when we reflect that they are brought about in the delicate organs of a comparatively feeble bird, under the influence of animal heat and the vital forces. They embrace a series of decomposing and recomposing operations which it is difficult to imitate in the laboratory. In the experiment to which allusion has been made, the amount of earthy material found in the eggs and the excrement of the hen exceeded that contained in the food she consumed. This seems paradoxical, and can only be explained upon the ground that birds as well as animals have the power, in times of exigency, of drawing upon their own bodies for material which is required to perform necessary functions.

The shell of an ordinary sized hen's egg weighs about 106 grains, that is, the inorganic portion of it; and if a bird lays 100 eggs in a year, she produces about 22 ounces of nearly pure carbonate of lime in that period of time, which would afford chalk enough to meet the wants of a farmer, or perhaps even of a house carpenter of moderate business, for a twelvemonth.

If a farmer has a flock of one hundred hens, they produce in egg-shells about 137 pounds of chalk annually; and yet not a pound of the substance, or perhaps not even an ounce, exists around the farm-house within the circuit of their feeding-ground. This is a source of lime production not usually recognized by farmers or hen-fanciers, and it is by no means insignificant. The materials of the manufacture are found in the food consumed, and in the sand, pebble-stones, brick-dust, bits of bones, etc., which hens and other birds are continually picking up from the earth. The instinct is keen for these apparently innutritious and refractory substances, and they are devoured with as eager a relish as the cereal grains or insects. If hens are confined to barns or out-buildings, it is obvious that the egg-producing machinery cannot be kept long in action, unless the materials for the shell are supplied in ample abundance.

Within the shell the animal portion of the egg is found, which consists of a viscous, colorless liquid called albumen, or the *white*, and a yellow, globular mass called the vitellus, or *yolk*. The white of the egg consists of two parts, each of which is enveloped in distinct membranes. The outer bag of albumen, next the shell, is quite a thin, watery body, while the next, which invests the yolk, is heavy and thick. But few housekeepers who break eggs ever distinguish between the *two whites*, or know of their existence even. Each has its appropriate office to fulfil during the progress of incubation or hatching, and one acts, in the mysterious process, as important a part as the other. If we remove this glairy fluid from the shell and place it in a glass, and plunge into it a strip of reddened litmus paper, a blue tinge is immediately produced, which indicates the presence of an alkali. The alkali is soda in a free condition, and its presence is of the highest consequence, for without it the liquid would be *insoluble*. A portion of the white of egg when diluted with water, and a few drops of vinegar or acetic acid added to it, undergoes a rapid change. The liquid becomes cloudy and flocculent, and small bits of shreddy matter fall to the bottom of the vessel. This is pure albumen, made so by removing the soda held in combination by the use of the acid. A pinch of soda added to the solid precipitate redissolves it, and it is again liquid. There is another way by which the albumen is rendered solid, and that is by the application of heat. Eggs placed in boiling-hot water pass from the soluble to the insoluble state quite rapidly, or in other words, the albumen both of the white and the yolk becomes "coagulated." No contrast can be greater than that between a boiled and unboiled egg. Not only is it changed physically, but there is a change in chemical properties, and yet no chemist can tell in what the change consists. It is true that water extracts a little alkali, and a trace of sulphide of sodium, but the abstraction of these bodies is hardly sufficient to account for the change in question.

The hardening of the albumen of egg by heat constitutes the cooking process, and this deserves a moment's consideration. Great as is the physical and chemical difference between a fully cooked and an uncooked egg, it is no less remarkable in the degree of digestibility conferred upon it by the process. Uncooked, it passes by the most simple processes of assimilation from the digestive to the nutritive and circulatory organs, and is at once employed in nourishing or sustaining the bodily functions. Unduly cooked, the egg resists the action of the gastric juices for a long time, and becomes unsuited to the stomachs of the weak and dyspeptic. A raw or soft-boiled egg is of all varieties of food the most concentrated and nourishing; a hard-boiled egg is apt to trouble the digestion of the strong and healthful, and its nutrient properties are sensibly impaired.

The yolk contains water and albumen, but associated with these is quite a large number of mineral and other substances which render it very complex in composition. The bright yellow color is due to a peculiar fat or oil, which is capable of reflecting the yellow rays of light, and this oil holds the sulphur and phosphorus which abound in the egg. If the yolk be removed and dried, and the yellow oil separated, it will be found to form two thirds of the substance. The whole weight in its natural state is about 300 grains, of which three fifths are water; of the white, more than three quarters are water.

The yolk and albumen of a fecundated egg remain as sweet and free from corruption during the whole time of incubation as they are in new-laid eggs, and there is but little loss of water; whereas an unfecundated egg passes rapidly into putrefactive decay and perishes.

Any one who eats three or four eggs at breakfast, consumes that number of embryo chicks. All the materials which enter into the legs, bones, feathers, bill, etc., of the new-born chick exist in the egg, as nothing is derived from outside. The little creature that has just pecked his way out of his calcareous prison-house, has lime and phosphorus in his bones, sulphur in his feathers, iron, potash, soda, and manganese in his blood, all of which mineral constituents came from the egg, and are taken into the stomach when it is eaten as food. The valuable or important salts are contained in the yolk, and hence this portion of the egg is the most useful in some forms of disease. A weakly person, in whom nerve force is deficient and the blood impoverished, may take the yolks of eggs with advantage. The iron and phosphoric compounds are in a condition to be readily assimilated, and although homeopathic in quantity, nevertheless exert a marked influence upon the system. The yolks of eggs, containing as they do less albumen, are not so injuriously affected by heat as the white, and a hard-boiled yolk

CHEMISTRY OF A HEN'S EGG. 27

may be usually eaten by invalids without inconvenience. The composition of a fresh egg, exclusive of the shell, may be presented as follows: —

Water	74 parts.
Albumen	14 "
Oil or fat	10.5 "
Mineral salts	1.5 "
	100

The whole usually weighs about a thousand grains, of which the shell makes a tenth part. The chick-making materials, exclusive of water, form only one quarter of the weight of the liquid contents, or only about 200 grains. This seems to be a small beginning upon which to rear the full-grown rooster. The bulk or quantity, as found in hens' eggs, and indeed in the eggs of all birds, is wonderfully disproportionate to the size of the mother bird. The laying of eggs must be regarded as a particularly exhausting process, and yet fowls will keep it up for a long time and not lose much in flesh. We have a hen of the *game* variety, which has recently laid 22 eggs in 22 consecutive days, and they average in weight 1,000 grains each. This gives in amount 22,000 grains, or rather more than three pounds avoirdupois, of which about two and a quarter pounds are water. The dozen or more ounces of rich nutritive material, parted with in 22 days, would seem to be a prodigious draught upon the small physical structure of the bird, but there were no indications of exhaustion.

Whilst it is true that the quickening of an egg, which results in the birth of a chick, is no more marvellous a process or result than the embryotic development of any creature endowed with the mysterious principle of life, yet there are some circumstances connected with it which make it a matter of greater perplexity and wonder. Here is an oval white body consisting of a calcareous shell, within which there are some semi-fluid substances, consisting mainly of albumen and water, without any signs of life. In fact there is no life; it is simply a mass of dead, inanimate matter. Talk as much as we will about the germinal principle involved in the structure of the egg, we are totally unable to recognize it, or form any conception of its nature. There is no evidence of the presence of any germ, or principle of life whatever. The egg left to itself decays like other organized substances, but with our assistance in simply transferring it to a place where the temperature is kept in a certain uniform condition, in a few weeks the albumen, water, oil, and mineral salts are transformed into a living chick, which thrusts its little beak through the shell, and in ten minutes is running about almost able to take care of itself. Here is the development of life apparently without the agency of the mother, and what a marvel! The chemist may place together in a body, in a warm place, just such elements or substances; he may carefully weigh the water, the albumen, the phosphatic compounds, the sulphur, the iron, soda, etc., and construct a very accurate egg mixture, but out of it all there will never come a living chick. In this we obtain some idea how little we actually know about *life*, how dark is the region where the life principle begins, or where the vital forces originate. The indefatigable man of science has pushed his inquiries close up to the boundary between the inanimate and the animate, but he has never been able to obtain the least glimpse of anything upon the *life* side of the line. However great may be our curiosity, our skill, or knowledge in this state of existence, there is not the least probability that we shall ever be able to endow matter with life, or know much more than we do at present of its origin or nature.

REBREATHED AIR.

IT is a matter of astonishment to those who understand the importance of a proper observance of the chemical and physiological laws connected with our existence, to observe how great abuse of these laws the system is capable of withstanding. Not a third of the race have any knowledge of, or regard for, the important sanitary rules upon which life and health depend. Men, women, and children, in all parts of the world, huddle together in narrow huts, cellars, and garrets, and breathe over and over again the corrupted air, subsisting at the same time upon the most unsubstantial and improper food; yet they manage to live out many weary days, and months, and even years, in these abodes.

The power of resistance to external and internal disturbing and destroying forces, possessed by the animal organism, is indeed marvellous. Great as is this power, however, and constant as is the warfare kept up by the vital forces against the unnatural and evil influences of bad air and bad food, the conflict is an unequal one. The inroads of disease cannot very long be resisted; the great fundamental laws upon which life and health depend cannot always be violated with impunity.

Among the many detrimental influences to which human beings are subjected, no one is greater than rebreathed air. Whilst there are tens of thousands who suffer through this agency involuntarily, there are other tens of thousands who might, if they would, escape from its baneful influence. There is bad air in churches, lecture-rooms, theatres, schoolrooms, parlors, bed-chambers, etc., which ought not to be present; or if, when occupied, the air of these rooms *must* become vitiated, then they ought never to be occupied. Certainly, enough has been written regarding ventilation to arouse public attention to its importance; but, after all, little heed is given to the matter in buildings, public or private.

Let us reflect a moment upon rebreathed air. What is it? It is, strictly speaking, one of the excrementitious products of the human organism. It is a mixture of gaseous bodies which have entered the system, been subjected to chemical changes, then rejected as a waste product.

Rebreathed air is the only excrementary matter thrown off by men or animals which is not positively abhorrent to all the senses; which is not cast away and shunned by all classes, — the ignorant and the learned, the cleanly and the uncleanly, the civilized and the savage. A delicate and fastidious lady will spend hours in a crowded theatre, ball-room, or lecture-room, and take into her lungs a gaseous mixture which has already traversed the air passages and impinged upon the lung cells of perhaps hundreds of men and women. If she should learn that her tooth-brush at any time had come in contact with the surfaces over which this air passed, it would be speedily cast aside, and a new one purchased.

But it is the chemical change which results in air when respired that renders it unfit for further use. It is reasonable to suppose — in fact, we know — that rebreathed air is little less than poison to the blood. Consumption and scrofula are found in intimate connection with imperfectly ventilated sleeping apartments, school-rooms, living-rooms, etc. A vigorous constitution may fight bravely and persistently against the influence of the poison; but the crash comes at last. No one can subsist for many years upon rebreathed air.

Animals suffer from it as unmistakably as man; and similar diseases are produced in them. The lions and tigers and bears and hyenas confined in menageries, kept close and warm, die speedily of consumption. True tubercle is produced; weakness, emaciation, death, results. It may be that the carbon is retained unoxidized, and that, by further chemical action, it is forced into new combinations by which bodies are formed of a poisonous nature, or which act the part of a ferment in the blood.

We do not know precisely *how* rebreathed air produces its deleterious influence, nor is it worth while to stop to inquire, in this discussion. It is certain that its effects are fatal to health. It would be absurd to assert that the frightful prevalence of consumption is due entirely to this agency; as all intelligent observers understand that there are many causes operating to produce or develop this disease. It is nevertheless probable that impure or rebreathed air is the greatest agent of evil in inducing, and rendering fatal, pulmonary affections. The crowded, badly-ventilated school-room is often the place where, early in life, rebreathed air commences its deadly work. Not one school-room in a hundred in this country is a fit place in which to confine children six or eight hours of the day. The little ones are herded together in a promiscuous crowd: those of tender years and those more advanced, the feeble and the strong, the sickly and the well, are all subjected to the same hours of study, the same school discipline, and all breathe the same deleterious air. The hardy and the strong may be able to resist the influence of the poison; the weak and tender ones grow pale and haggard, and, struggling on through their school-days, live perhaps to the age of puberty, and then drop into the consumptive's grave. Will parents never awake to the enormity of this evil?

Small, ill-ventilated sleeping-rooms, in which re-breathed air is ever present, are nurseries of consumption. These are not found alone in cities and large towns, or among the poor and lowly. Well-to-do farmers' daughters and sons in the country, — those who live among the mountains of the New England States, where God's pure air is wholly undefiled, — are often victims of consumption. How is this explained? Look into their bedrooms; examine into their daily habits of life; and the cause is made plain. Old-fashioned fireplaces are boarded up; rubber window-strips and stoves have found their way into the most retired nooks and corners of the land; and the imprisoned mountain air in country dwellings is heated to a high point, and breathed over and over during the days and nights of the long winter months. It is certainly true that girls in the country take less exercise in the open air than those residing in cities. They appear to be more *afraid* of pure, cold air than city girls. Consumption is not less rare among females in the country than in cities, in the present age. It was not so formerly. The declarations of grandmothers and old physicians go to show that, fifty years ago, consumption was hardly known in the rural districts. The winds whistled through the dwellings then, and the fire blazed and roared upon the hearth. Half the time, in the cold winters, "the backs of the inmates were freezing, while the front parts of the person were roasting;" and yet there was less rheumatism than now, and no consumption.

Whilst we have made changes in dwellings, workshops, and public buildings, which operate to sadly deteriorate and confine the interior air, the outside atmosphere is just as pure, just as healthful, as in the days of our ancestors. Let us adopt means to secure a full measure of this "pabulum of life," clear, undiluted, uncontaminated, day and night, during the hours of sleep and study. Let us live as much as we possibly can in the *open air*, and the measure of health will be greatly increased, and life prolonged.

CHEMISTRY OF A CIGAR.

WHEN Columbus, three hundred and seventy-five years ago, landed upon that verdant island of the tropics which proved the gateway to a new world, he was struck with the strange habits and customs of the people who flocked about him. Probably no one of these habits excited his pity or disgust more than that which was seen to prevail among both sexes, of rolling together the dried leaves of a plant offensive in taste and odor, placing them in their mouths, and inhaling the smoke. If he had been told that, within two or three centuries, not only the descendants of those who comprised the Christian and polished court under whose auspices his bold enterprise was undertaken, but the whole civilized world would be imitating the savages in the seemingly filthy practice, he would have ridiculed the idea as one most improbable and preposterous. The prediction would have proved a true one. The taste of the poor Indians for tobacco was certainly not peculiar to them; and wonderful is the fact, that, the more advanced, Christianized, and enlightened mankind have become, the larger the increase in the consumption of this pungent, narcotic Indian weed. In the time of the great navigator the plant was found growing wild upon the heights of the island; and not until a full century had elapsed did it become the object of care and cultivation. It was introduced into Europe, and, in spite of the edicts and anathemas thundered against it by popes and kings, its use rapidly increased, until it became well-nigh universal. King James, in his celebrated "Counterblast to Tobacco," denounced the smoking of cigars as "a custom loathsome to the eye, hateful to the nose, harmful to the brain, dangerous to the lungs, and, in the black, stinking fume thereof, nearest resembling the horrible stygian smoake of the pit that is bottomless." Pope Urban VIII. issued a bull against it. The Russian Government threatened with death all found puffing a second cigar. The Sultan of Turkey declared smoking a sin against the religion of the Prophet. In fact, tobacco came under the ban of the powers, temporal and spiritual, of the whole world; and yet, altogether, they utterly failed to suppress its use.

What is the nature of the plant whose history is so extraordinary? What strange elements enter into its composition? What is the *chemistry* of those leaves which, when rolled into cylindrical form, constitute the cigar, so highly cherished by millions of smokers in all parts of the habitable globe?

Tobacco belongs to a suspicious and exceedingly dangerous order of plants — the *solanaceæ*, or *nightshades*. The deadly nightshade, henbane, thorn apple, belong to this order, and all are powerful narcotic poisons. It is true that to its *genera* belong the edible potato and tomato; but we must remember that even the potato is possessed of poisonous narcotic properties, which are only rendered harmless by cooking. To the farmer who cultivates tobacco, it proves a robber of the first magnitude. It possesses a capacity for plundering the soil greater than that of any other tree, shrub, or plant known; the amount of mineral constituents which it carries off can be judged of by carefully examining the ash, as it accumulates upon the end of the ignited cigar. It often remains after the organic portion is removed, showing the full size and outline of the rolled leaves, and to the eye apparently nothing is lost by combustion. If the wood burned in our stoves and upon our hearths was as rich in soil constituents, we should need the services of extra servants to carry away the ashes. Every one hundred pounds of the dried leaves which the soil produces, rob it of at least twenty pounds of its most valuable mineral atoms. In the exportation of tobacco, immense quantities of the richest soil of Cuba and other tobacco producing countries are transported to distant lands, and scattered to the wind and the storm. The impoverishment thus produced must be met, on the part of the cultivator, by heavy expenditures for fertilizers; else, a few years only suffice to reduce lands, through its agency, to barren wastes. The plant is hungry for potash, and of this it consumes large quantities. In every one hundred pounds of the dried leaves, there is contained nearly five of this alkali. A bushel of ashes, such as form upon the end of the smoker's cigar, would, if leached, and the ley formed into soap, make enough to serve the purposes of a small family for a year.

It is a common belief that cigar ashes constitute an excellent and safe detergent or dentifrice for the teeth; and many smokers are in the habit of saving and applying them to this purpose. The strong alkaline nature of the ash, acting in conjunction with the silica in its finely subdivided condition, would certainly afford cleansing properties of a high order; and unless the alkali is too caustic for frequent use, its employment in this direction can hardly be condemned.

The comparative exhaustive effects of tobacco upon soils may be judged of from the fact that fourteen tons of wheat, fifteen tons of corn, twelve tons of oats, remove no more of the principles of fertility than a single ton of tobacco. The activity of chemical forces, therefore, necessary in the growth of the plant, must be exceedingly great; and the curious and complex character of the vitalized structure stamps it as among the most extraordinary pertaining to the vegetable kingdom. Aside from the ash constituents, the chemistry of a cigar, in respect to agents directly influencing the animal economy, is the same as the chemistry of tobacco in any form. The chemical agents contained in tobacco are brought in contact with the same tissues and mucous surfaces, whether the form be that of smoke, as in smoking, or aqueous extract, as in chewing, or of substance finely divided, as in snuff-taking.

Tobacco and tobacco smoke contain three important and distinguishing chemical agents, which confer upon them peculiar properties. If we take a common glass retort and affix to it a condenser, and place in the retort a pound of fresh tobacco leaves with a pint of water, upon applying heat and distilling, a minute quantity of volatile oil comes over and floats on the water in the receiver. This has a pungent odor, and appears to be the aroma, or condensed essence of the plant. When held to the nose, it causes violent sneezing; and, if placed on the tongue, the whole of the mouth and throat seems to be instantly pervaded with the strong taste of tobacco. To the smoker, this principle is most important, as it is the one upon which the peculiar and gratifying taste of the smoke depends. It is changed or ripened by age, or modified, in the growth of the plant, by soil and climate. The amount of this wonderful principle in a cigar is truly homœopathic. In one of ordinary size there is not more than the twentieth part of a grain; and yet it pervades every fibre and every atom of every leaf. Extract or remove it from the cigar, and instantly it becomes worthless and repulsive to the smoker. This illustrates how marvellously minute are the ingredients upon which the sensible properties or peculiar action of many medicinal agents depend.

If we repeat the experiment with the pound of tobacco leaves in the retort, modifying or changing the action by pouring in a few drops of sulphuric acid and half an ounce of caustic soda, previous to distilling, there will come over a colorless, oily liquid, which sinks to the bottom of the receiver. This is essentially the *nicotine*, or the acrid, burning, poisonous principle of tobacco. By further manipulation, it can be formed into crystals; but they cannot long be retained in that state. This is the *prussic acid* of tobacco — an agent so terribly destructive to animal life that a single drop, placed upon the tongue of a dog, instantly produces asphyxia and death. A few grains placed upon a stove and volatilized, in a church or theatre, will produce distressing cough and asthma simultaneously upon thousands of people. The one hundredth part of a grain, pricked into the skin with a pin, will produce giddiness, nausea, and fainting. This poison exists in tobacco in the proportion of from *two* to *nine* pounds in one hundred of the dried leaves, the quantity varying in tobacco grown upon different soils.

A consideration of these facts regarding nicotine is well calculated to surprise and alarm every smoker. There is no exaggeration in the statement; but we must remember that nicotine does not exist in tobacco in a free state. It is called by chemists an *alkaloidal principle*, and found in tobacco in chemical combination with an acid. The acid is identical with the malic, found in fruits; but in tobacco it is called *nicotic* acid. The virulence of nicotine is considerably modified not only by its association with the acid which it holds, but probably by the presence of the other substances. Modified, however, as it is, it confers upon tobacco poisonous properties of a most extraordinary character.

The third distinguishing chemical agent which tobacco contains, is an *empyreumatic* oil, which is obtained when the cured leaves are distilled in connection with high-pressure-steam. Foxglove (*Digitalis purpurea*), another of the poisonous plants, affords an oil by distillation, which strongly resembles that from tobacco. The oil is acrid, pungent, disagreeable, and poisonous, and contains much nicotine. If the reader wishes to try an experiment, to learn the nature of this oil, let him procure the bowl of an old tobacco-pipe,* or cigar-tube, and scrape off a small portion of the moist "soot," or pound up a bit of the pipe no larger than a kernel of corn, inclose in meat, and throw it to a cat. Death will probably occur in less than five minutes. There are thousands of pipes in constant use among laborers, which contain oil enough to kill a dozen cats, and which are so "strong" that a person unused to tobacco could not fill the mouth once with the smoke passed through them, without experiencing the most unpleasant effects.

No matter in what form tobacco is used, whether it be in smoking, snuff-taking, or chewing, this volatile oil must come in intimate and constant contact with the mucous surfaces of the mouth and air-passages, and therefore, by absorption, a portion passes into the system. To what extent this absorptive process is carried, it is impossible to know with certainty. Probably it is very small in the case of those who use tobacco in moderation. The smoker usually entertains the idea that, in simply inhaling the smoke, contact with the active principles of tobacco is almost entirely obviated; but this is manifestly a mistake. The smoke holds these principles in a volatilized or minutely subdivided form, and they impinge upon all the absorbent vessels of the mouth.

If any one doubts the nature of the smoke, let him take a fine, clean, linen handkerchief, and, holding it to the mouth, force the smoke from a cigar through it several times. The palpable yellow hue imparted is due to the oil and volatile principles of tobacco held in the smoke. A good cigar, chemically considered, should contain a large portion of *nicotianine*, or the true aromatic essence, and a small portion of the poisonous *nicotine*. Different soils impart to the tobacco-leaf these principles in varying proportions. That of Cuba, and some other of the West India Islands, supplies the rich aroma in abundance, and but comparatively little nicotine. The tobacco from these sources is much sought after by smokers in all parts of the world, and the prices paid for it are enormous.

It is surprising how much tobacco is consumed daily by some smokers. Instances are not rare in which ten cigars are converted into smoke and ashes during each twenty-four hours of the year, by men of not strong constitutions. Let us see how much of the poisonous principle of tobacco, *nicotine*, is imbibed in the smoke of these cigars. The finest Cuba tobacco contains at least two per cent. of the alkaloid; and assuming that each cigar weighs sixty grains, ten would weigh six hundred grains. In this amount of tobacco there would be twelve grains of pure, crystallizable nicotine. This is volatilized by heat, drawn into the mouth along with the other organized principles, and a considerable portion mingles with the saliva, and impinges upon the exposed mucous surfaces. The twelve grains isolated, made into aqueous solution, and taken into the stomachs, or injected into the subcutaneous vessels of three strong men, would probably, in three or five minutes, deprive them of life. A crystal, weighing two grains, placed under the tongue of a healthy adult person, and allowed to dissolve and become absorbed, would also produce fatal consequences. It will be easy for those of our readers who smoke two, three, or more cigars a day, to estimate from the above calculation how much nicotine they convert into smoke in the twenty-four hours.

We are considering the cigar strictly from a chemical point of view, and therefore do not intend to be betrayed into the expression of extended or dogmatic opinions regarding the hygienic influence of tobacco upon the human system. There are plenty of sensational preachers and reformers who think themselves wise enough to enlighten smokers and chewers upon this point.

It must be confessed that chemists, as well as many others, are puzzled to know how a plant so utterly repulsive to the natural sense came to possess the power of playing the tyrant with human appetites. It is a still greater puzzle, however, to understand how tens of thousands of people, of all classes, ages, and conditions, are able to masticate, smoke, and snuff the substance of the plant, and not suffer the most serious inroads upon the health. It is obvious that all cannot use tobacco without much physical disturbance. Upon the writer, its use in any form, even in small quantities, is followed by the usual alarming effects of the narcotic poisons.

There is evidently design in the marvellous adjustment of the chemical atoms which give to the tobacco leaf its singular properties. It is unlike anything else which the vegetable kingdom is capable of producing. Mankind cannot be persuaded to roll up leaves of any other plant and smoke them, as they do tobacco. Neither chemists nor physicians are able to point out any very useful purpose to which the plant can be applied. The former may go to it for a supply of the peculiar alkaloidal principle, *nicotine*, but this substance is only useful in destroying troublesome insects and animals. A cheaper and equally potent poison is found in the *nux vomica*, strychnine. In medicine it serves no useful end not obtainable through other agents. It must be admitted that there are many vegetable productions which, so far as our knowledge extends, are valueless, or which neither contribute to the sustentation of life, nor avert disease, nor add, in any way, to our well-being or happiness. Tobacco, perhaps, should not be ranked with them; for, while it is in no respect essential to existence, it does seem to add to the *happiness* of a large portion of mankind. Fight against it as we may, brand it as a poison as we certainly *must*, still the smoke of a million cigars will curl upward every day, and the expectorating crowd of chewers will continue to soil our carpets, and render our railway cars and hotels almost unendurable.

CHEMISTRY OF A PINT OF KEROSENE.

THERE is scarcely an article, solid or fluid, which is more generally regarded in this country as one of household necessity, than what is known as kerosene. It is brought to the cities, from the oil regions, in vast quantities, and from thence is distributed to every town and village throughout the country. Storekeepers arrange it for sale in close proximity with sugars, coffee, tea, and flour; and often the dark, moist, and odorous casks are seen mounted by the side of calicoes and ribbons.

The tallow candle and oil lamp no longer flicker and shed their dim light in dwelling or workshop. A more intense and diffusive light now flashes through the windows, and penetrates far into the surrounding darkness. The country lad or dame, visiting the city, is no longer dazzled and bewildered by the blaze of gas-lights; the home far away among the hills is illuminated by rays equally brilliant, and the eye has long since become accustomed to the glare. Kerosene must be considered among the wonderful things which have been developed by this progressive age, and its history and nature worthy of examination and study.

The name, "kerosene," is rather a fanciful one. It originated with one of the early manufacturers, and has now come to possess a general significance. It is applied not only to the oil distilled from coals, but to the illuminating liquid which comes from rock-oil, or petroleum. It is needful that this important body should have a name, generally understood and adopted; and perhaps the word "kerosene" is as good as any that could be suggested.

Before the discovery of petroleum, kerosene was manufactured from soft or bituminous coals by a peculiar process of distillation. The statement seems paradoxical, or contradictory, that there is not a particle of oil, or gas, or naphtha, in a lump of this variety of coal, when it is known that from it the chemist not only produces them in large quantities, but a dozen or more other bodies, of very remarkable and diverse natures. A lump of coal is capable of yielding olefiant or illuminating gas, hydrogen, sulphydric acid, sulphurous acid, ammonia, kerosene, kerosolene, benzine, benzoline, naphtha, naphthaline, paraffine, creosote, carbolic acid, tar, pitch, asphaltum, and some other substances; and yet, as isolated bodies, most of these cannot be said to exist at all in the coal. Their production is due to the manipulating processes to which the coal is subjected. Heat is the great disorganizer which breaks up, or separates, the atoms of carbon, hydrogen, nitrogen, sulphur, etc., and forces them into new combinations. Most of these substances are of a very remarkable character, and largely employed in medicine and the arts. The gaseous bodies are used for lighting, heating, bleaching, etc. Ammonia is used for a great variety of purposes, and is almost indispensable in some processes or manufactures. Very nearly all the ammonia consumed, amounting to many thousands of pounds, is manufactured from the waste products of gas-works, or indirectly from coal. Benzine, benzoline, gasoleine, kerosolene, naphtha (all of which may be included in the general term *naphtha*), are extremely light hydrocarbon liquids, of a similar nature, but differing in density and volatility. Kerosolene, or rhigolene, is the lightest and most volatile of all known liquids. It boils violently when exposed upon a warm day in summer. Its specific gravity is 0.625. Benzine is employed for making the beautiful aniline dyes, now so popular. The gorgeous rainbow tints derivable from coal may be regarded as the stored-up sunshine of a past geological epoch; and the science and skill of our advanced age have proved adequate for its liberation or isolation. It is a curious fact that the benzole obtained from petroleum cannot be converted into nitro-benzole, and thence into dye colors. The liquid physically resembles that resulting from the distillation of coal; but, chemically, it widely differs. Creosote and carbolic acid possess remarkable antiseptic or preserving properties. Putrefactive change in organized bodies is instantly arrested by the presence of carbolic acid; and hence, this newly discovered agent promises to be of the highest importance to the human family.

Perhaps no one of the results of the chemical manipulation of soft coals is more striking, or awakens greater wonder in the popular mind, than the production of that beautiful, snowy white substance, used so largely in the manufacture of candles, — paraffine. Naphthaline is still more beautiful. It is produced in the form of scales or crystals, and resembles the pearl or opal in color or appearance. How bodies physically so dissimilar can come from black, dirty coals, is a fact almost incomprehensible to those unacquainted with technical chemistry; and, indeed, we cannot wonder it is so. When the farmer is told that the chemist is able to change not only a lump of coal, but the moist, black "peat" from his meadow, into oil or candles adapted to light his dwelling, he is perhaps ready to admit the truthfulness of the statement; but *how* so strange a transmutation is effected is a problem deeply puzzling.

The changes in coals and carbonaceous substances, which result in the production of oily liquids, are effected by a process called destructive distillation. If water is placed in a retort or still, and heat applied, the particles are raised in the form of vapor, and by condensation are resolved back again into water. There is no change effected in the liquid. But, if we place soft coals in an iron retort, and apply heat, they are disorganized or destroyed. No coal can be found in the retort, or in any vessel containing the volatilized products, after the operation is completed. The *degree* of heat applied will determine whether it be resolved into gaseous bodies, or into liquids and semi-solids. If a cherry-red heat be kept up during the distillation, we have, as a chief product from the coal, olefiant or illuminating gas; if a lower, or dull red heat, little gas comes over, but copious vapors, which, when condensed, form a thick, black, greasy fluid, of a not very inviting character. This fluid is made up of a great number of substances, the four most important being kerosene oil for burning, oil for lubricating, paraffine, and naphtha. To obtain the pure kerosene oil, the liquid is subjected to several more distillations, in which strong sulphuric acid is employed to aid in the purification, and the acid is afterwards removed by caustic soda. Our limits are too narrow to describe the processes for obtaining the paraffine and other substances, or to enter into details regarding the manufacture of kerosene. The brief statement made will serve to convey a general idea of the methods adopted to convert soft coals into kerosene oil.

In manufacturing kerosene from petroleum, the processes are essentially the same. We must regard the crude petroleum as representing the black, tarry liquid obtained from the first distillation of coal.

In the use of petroleum, this first process is saved; the coal having probably been distilled in a far back geological period, on a gigantic scale, by some processes of nature not well understood. The vast cavities in the rocks in which this crude product is stored represent, as oil reservoirs, the cisterns in which the manufacturer stored the first products of his coal retorts, before the discovery of petroleum. As soon as this discovery was made, the production of kerosene from coals was promptly suspended, as no one could compete against a natural product existing in immense quantities, which had already passed one important stage of its manufacture.

In the distillation of coal a substance is left in the retorts, called *coke*, which is very nearly pure carbon. In chemical composition this corresponds with our hard or anthracite coals. By no possible manipulation can a drop of kerosene be obtained from coke, or from anthracite coal; they are both *residuums*, or results of an exhaustive chemical change. The anthracite coal-beds may be regarded as the coke, remaining after the distillatory process, which produced petroleum, was completed. Artificial coke, by pressure and moisture, can be made to resemble anthracite in its physical aspects. A vast number of interesting questions arise at this point regarding the probable origin of petroleum, its nature, and distribution; but we must hasten to consider the chemical changes to which a pint of kerosene is subjected after being placed in a lamp and burned as a source of artificial illumination.

Kerosene is a pure hydrocarbon liquid; that is, a liquid made up of the elements hydrogen and carbon. Both of these are combustible, or possess a strong affinity for oxygen; and associated together, as in kerosene, they afford a luminous flame when burned by uniting with oxygen. The results, or products, of combustion differ in no respect from those which proceed from other organized carbonaceous bodies, being mainly water and carbonic acid.

Estimating carefully the amount of light afforded by a measured quantity of kerosene, and contrasting it, in price, with gas, sperm oil, wax candles,

CHEMISTRY OF A PINT OF KEROSENE. 55

etc., it is found to be far less costly than either; and it is so convenient and cleanly that its discovery must be regarded as a blessing to the race.

So much has been said respecting the *explosive* nature of kerosene, this point demands consideration. A general impression prevails among consumers that kerosene is *explosive*, and its use attended with a considerable amount of danger. Such, however, is not the case; it is no more explosive than water; and the employment of properly prepared oil is safe under all ordinary conditions. It is important that there should be a clear understanding of the nature of kerosene, the cause of accidents, and the conditions under which they occur.

As has been stated, kerosene is not explosive. A lighted taper may be thrust into it, or flame applied in any way, and it does not explode. On the contrary, it extinguishes flame, if experimented with at the usual temperatures of our rooms. Kerosene accidents occur from two causes: first, imperfect manufacture of the article; second, adulterations. An imperfectly manufactured oil is that which results when the distillation has been carried on at too low a temperature, and a part of the naphtha remains in it. Adulterations are largely made by unprincipled dealers, who add twenty or thirty per cent. of naphtha after it leaves the manufacturer's hands. The light naphthas which have been spoken of as known in commerce under the names of benzine, benzoline, gasoleine, etc., are very volatile, inflammable, and dangerous. They, however, in themselves, are not explosive; neither are they, when placed in lamps, capable of furnishing any *gas* which is explosive. Accidents of this nature are due entirely to the facility with which *vapor* is produced from them at low temperatures. But the vapor by itself is inexplosive; to render it so, *it must be mixed with air*. A lamp may be filled with bad kerosene, or with the vapor even, and in no possible way can it detonate, or explode, unless atmospheric air has somehow got mixed with the vapor. A lamp, therefore, full, or nearly full of the liquid is safe; and also one full of pure warm vapor is safe. Explosions generally occur when the lamp is first lighted without being filled, and also late in the evening, when the fluid is nearly exhausted. The reason of this will readily be seen. In using imperfect or adulterated kerosene, the space above the line of oil is always filled with vapor; and so long as it is warm, and rising freely, no air can reach it, and it is safe. At bedtime, when the family retire, the light is extinguished; the lamp cools, a portion of the vapor is condensed; this creates a partial vacuum in the space, which is instantly filled with air. The mixture is now more or less explosive; and when, upon the next evening, the lamp is lighted without replenishing with oil, as is often done, an explosion is liable to take place. Late in the evening, when the oil is nearly consumed, and the space above filled with vapor, the lamp cannot explode so long as it remains at rest upon the table. But take it in hand, agitate it, carry it into a cool room, the vapor is cooled, air passes in, and the mixture becomes explosive. A case of lamp explosion came to the writer's knowledge a few years since, which was occasioned by taking a lamp from the table to answer a ring at the door-bell. The cool outside air, which impinged upon the lamp in the hands of the lady, rapidly condensed the vapor, air passed in, and an explosion occurred, which resulted fatally. If the lamp had been full of fluid, this accident could not have occurred. Before carrying it to the door, flame might have been thrust into the lamp with safety; the vapor would have ignited, but no explosion could have taken place.

This brief explanation will serve to show the *cause* of lamp explosions. We hear much said about dangerous *gases* being formed in lamps, but this is an error. In burning the most dangerous kinds of kerosene, no decomposition takes place, resulting in the formation of explosive gases. The whole hazard comes from air-mixed vapor.

But how can we be positively assured of safety in the use of kerosene? How can we know of the quality or character of the article offered us by dealers? These are important questions, which will naturally arise in the mind of the reader. We answer, there is *positive* assurance of safety, if pure, well manufactured kerosene is consumed. We do not believe a serious accident ever occurred from kerosene, the inflammable point of which was above 110° F., and this is the legal standard. During the past fifteen years the writer has made a large number of experiments upon burning fluids, and investigated thoroughly the conditions under which accidents occur in their use. Personal investigation has been made of the alleged cases of explosions, many of which have been reported, and therefore opinions are expressed upon the subject with a confident feeling of their correctness.

Purchases made direct, of long established, reputable manufacturers, afford assurances of safety. But such are not readily accessible, and in most cases a supply is sought from the nearest dealer, without any definite knowledge of the source from whence it comes, or its character or quality. If consumers are willing to be put to a little trouble, a simple experiment will determine the safety of the kerosene they purchase. Fill a pint bowl two thirds full of boiling water, and into it put a common metallic thermometer. The temperature will run up to over 200°. By gradually adding cold water, bring down the temperature of the water to 110°, and then pour into the bowl a spoonful of the kerosene, and apply a lighted match. If it takes fire, the article should be rejected as dangerous; if not, it may be used with a confident feeling of its safety. In this experiment, which is the most simple that can be devised, the fire test is directly applied. Upon practical trials it has been found to afford correct results.

There are severe enactments, both state and national, against the sale of kerosene of a dangerous character; but, as in the case of many other articles subjected to adulterating processes, the fear of the law does not deter from sophistication. Kerosene is largely mixed with the cheap naphthas to reduce the cost, and thus the lives of consumers are jeopardized.

We would caution our readers against another form of fraud and deception. There are many men in all the large towns and cities, engaged in compounding and vending burning fluids under various names, alleged to be safer, or cheaper, or better, than kerosene. Chemical examination of many of these fluids proves them to be either dangerous mixtures of oil and naphtha, or kerosene with a little coloring matter added. Avoid all "chemical oils," "lunar oils," "oleines," etc.; from the nature of the case they must be fraudulent, as there are no liquid or solid bodies known to science which furnish perfect artificial light so cheaply as kerosene, the product of crude petroleum.

THE LOST ARTS.

MUCH has been said regarding the lost arts; and a general impression prevails that there were many wonderful processes, arts, and contrivances known to the ancients which have been lost to us. Is this idea correct? Is it true that the old Egyptians, Grecians, and Romans were our superiors in any kind or branch of knowledge? Did they excel us in any department of art or mechanical labor? From a somewhat thorough examination of the treasures of ancient art found in the museums of Europe, and from a careful study of the works of the writers of antiquity, especially Pliny, who is the acknowledged source from which very much of this kind of information is drawn, the conclusion is reached that there is great looseness and exaggeration in the statements of those who have taken the affirmative of these questions.

It would be absurd to say that there were not some arts or processes belonging to the ancient civilization which have been lost, or are now imperfectly understood; but that the number is large, or that, if known, they would be of any importance to us, are points we are unwilling to admit. A considerable number of the elegant and useful arts which are so pleasing and essential to our comfort and happiness were undoubtedly known to the ancients; and this is indeed remarkable. We are not, however, in any sense indebted to them for a knowledge of these, as they have been rediscovered through the instrumentality of modern genius and research. We had none of their models to imitate: they have been secured to us through independent thought and skill. We have reinvented and rediscovered nearly or quite everything wonderful or useful known to the early races. And how vast and amazing the triumphs of modern science and discovery in directions entirely unknown and unsuspected by them!

No fact is more apparent than that human ingenuity, when directed by culture and intelligence, runs in certain specific channels, and is made competent to construct such devices and appliances as the age demands; or, perhaps we may say, just such as are most convenient and indispensable to the existing civilization. Thus the civilization of the old Roman world demanded, in the working of wood, planes, saws, squares, levels, bits, augers, hammers; the workers in iron and other metals required forges, blast-furnaces, anvils, tongs, sledge-hammers, punches, dies, etc.; the farmers wanted sickles, pruning-knives, hoes, shovels, spades, forks, ploughs, harrows; the warriors, shields, swords, spears, battle-axes, crossbows, and javelins. These the inventive faculty of the age was competent and prompt to supply. The artisans went on through successive ages, manufacturing and improving upon these implements, until they reached that degree of perfection which is so clearly shown and illustrated in discoveries at Herculaneum and Pompeii. In a considerable number of instances they reached the highest stage of perfection in the mechanic arts; at least, we are led to adopt this view, as, with all our modern science and skill, we are unable to make any essential improvements. Their planes, sickles, shovels, spades, hammers, saws, knives, swords, and a hundred other articles, in *form* and *construction*, were almost precisely like those in use among us at the present time. How has this happened?

During the dark ages which have intervened since the downfall of the Roman civilization, all knowledge of the form and construction of these implements was lost; and our devices must be, as before stated, original inventions. We knew nothing regarding the *form* of a Roman plane, or sickle, or spade, until Pompeii was disentombed, about a hundred years ago. When these discoveries were made, our inventors and artisans were amazed to find that, seventeen centuries since, the same forms of tools and implements were in the hands of husbandmen and workers in wood, iron, and stone. There is a limit to human skill as well as to human thought, and the same culture and ingenuity will reach about the same ends in any and every age. The ancient Grecians and Romans attained the limit of perfection in several departments of art; we have reached the same end in a much larger number. And it is reasonable to infer that, if our civilization was destroyed, and ages of barbarism should intervene before a new one arose, the ground which inventors, artists, and men of science have gone over in this age would once more be travelled; and if the same degree of civilization was attained, the same mechanical inventions and arts would again be reproduced.

Let us examine a few of the different branches or departments of the mechanical or industrial arts as practised by the ancient Romans, with the view of ascertaining if they possessed any processes not known to us, or if they excelled us in the products of their skill. It is alleged by some popular writers and lecturers that in the art of glass-making they were greatly our superiors. In proof of this they quote largely from the gossiping Pliny, and present his statements regarding the production of specimens so perfect and beautiful they could not be distinguished from precious stones. He mentions artificial hyacinths, sapphires, and emeralds, and a kind of black glass, which closely resembled the obsidian stone. It is certain that great excellence was reached in this department, as in one of the collections of antiquities at Rome imitations of chrysolite and emerald are shown, which are very perfect. They have not the smallest blemish, either externally or internally, and the colors are faultless. In coloring glass the ancients must have been acquainted with the metallic oxides, as they offer the only pigments capable of withstanding the intense heat required in glass fusions. They colored glass so perfectly, and imitated gems so successfully, that the hucksters and cheats of those times were able to deceive even the wives of the emperors. For Trebellius Pollio informs us of the whimsical way in which Gallienus punished an adventurous wretch who sold his wife a piece of glass for a jewel. Granted that they manufactured some excellent or even remarkable specimens of glass; that they gave tints most exquisite; that they made costly vessels, or drinking-cups, tables, vases, or even panelled rooms with it, — what did they more than we? Do we not make gems so perfect as to deceive those most experienced? Are not two thirds of the *brilliants* that refract light so beautifully in the bracelets and rings worn by modern ladies constructed simply of glass? Have we not made an imitation of the great Kohinoor diamond so perfect that, by the eye, it cannot be distinguished from the original? As regards colors, no specimens of ancient glass excel, or even compare with those produced in the present century. The brilliancy of our tints and their permanency have never been surpassed. But what of the *malleable glass* of the ancients? We do not believe any such glass was ever produced. The statements of Dion Cassius and Petronius Arbiter regarding the production of ductile glass by a celebrated Roman architect, are probably only other versions of the story told by Pliny regarding the artificer who, for making the same discovery, had his workshop demolished by a mob, who feared it would lower the value of gold, silver, and brass. The story is, that a vessel of this glass was brought into the presence of the Emperor Tiberius by the discoverer, and dashed upon the floor without breaking, the effect of the blow only indenting or bruising it a little. The inventor then took a hammer from his pocket and beat it out into its original shape, as if it had been made of thin metal. This is absurd. Glass is a vitrified substance; and it is now, and always has been, impossible to associate with it the property of malleability.

The glass of the ancients, like our own, was a

true silicate of soda, or potassa, and any substance constructed of other materials could not properly be called glass. It is possible for modern chemists to prepare, from some of the metals or metallic salts, a ductile material having a glossy appearance, which might pass for glass. From the fusion of chloride of silver a substance of this kind is formed, which, among the unscientific Romans, would readily be called glass. If they possessed the art of *spinning* glass, of which there is no evidence, vessels might have been constructed which would be flexible, and admit of being dashed upon the floor without breaking; but no bottle or vessel capable of holding liquids could be thus constructed. The writer has in his possession a card plate, procured of the glass-workers of Venice, made of glass in this form, which is a wonderful specimen of ingenuity and skill. It can be bent and thrown about without breaking, but *hammering* would soon reduce it to powder. In all that pertains to glass manufactures, — in the vastness of the production, cheapness, quality, colors, variety of forms and uses, we have made great advances over any race or races that have preceded us.

In the working of metals, in the various combinations and alloys formed, and in chemical treatment, we may justly claim a like superiority. Iron, although well known, was comparatively but little used among the ancient Romans, Grecians, Egyptians, etc. They did not understand easy processes for working it, and consequently articles constructed of iron bore a very high price. The iron ores of England were undoubtedly worked by the Romans, in the first centuries of the Christian era, as heaps of scoriæ, the refuse of their bloomaries, occur in various localities. Their processes of reduction were very simple, consisting of the deoxidation of the ore and the cementation of the metal by long-continued heat. They were not very far in advance of some of the ignorant tribes who now work iron in the interior of Africa.

We have no positive evidence that the ancients were acquainted with more than seven of the metals. Their list embraced copper, iron, gold, silver, lead, quicksilver, and tin. How insignificant this appears in contrast with the noble list of more than fifty metals known to us! Copper and its alloys were their favorite metals. They certainly knew as much regarding bronze, its composition and working, as we do. The enormous statue of the sun, known by the name of the Colossus of Rhodes, was composed entirely of this compound metal. It was indeed a huge structure, one hundred and five feet high, with legs spread, so that ships could pass between. There is no evidence that the legs extended across the harbor of Rhodes, although that is the popular idea. Chares, a celebrated artificer, spent twelve years in constructing it, and Pliny says that there were few that could clasp its thumb. A spiral staircase led to its summit, from whence might be descried Syria, and the ships proceeding to Egypt, in a great mirror suspended to the neck of the statue. It was overthrown by an earthquake, B. C. 224, and the fragments lay on the ground for nine hundred and twenty-three years, when they were sold by the Saracens to a Jew, who loaded nine hundred camels with the brass, A. D. 672. This was one of the wonders of the world; and vast as would be the undertaking, it is certain that modern skill would construct a like image in one fourth the time it took to construct this, if the large sum of money requisite could be supplied. The statue of St. Charles Borromeo, at Arona, Italy, is sixty-six feet high, composed of brass. This is the largest statue existing in the world. We have found that the *nose* of this statue afforded a very spacious and comfortable seat after a tedious climb to that high elevation. Immense quantities of copper and tin must have been mined by the ancients, as we are informed by Pliny that Rhodes alone was adorned by no less than one thousand colossal statues of the Sun in bronze, and Rome and all the large cities of the empire were filled with them. How can we account for the almost complete disappearance of these many thousands of tons of bronze?

It is generally supposed that the ancients were acquainted with a method of hardening copper, so as to make it subserve the purposes of iron and steel in the working of wood and stone. If this be true, the art is a lost one, as we certainly are ignorant of any such process. It is, however, hardly probable or possible that this supposition can be strictly true. Modern alloys of copper have been made of great hardness, but nothing that possessed the characteristics of steel. The sword-blades, spear-heads, hatchets, and cutting instruments of the ancients were probably only alloys of copper and tin, which were capable of meeting many wants in the absence of the harder and more refined ferruginous metals. It is, indeed, a mystery how they could, with the implements of metal at their command, construct such stupendous works of solid masonry, the remains of which are now seen in all parts of the Old World. They worked in the hardest stone apparently with as much facility as we do with our steel hammers, drills, and bars. The mystery, however, connected with metallic hand implements is no greater than that regarding the mechanical appliances by which such huge masses of solid rock were detached from the mountain sides, and transported long distances. They had no gunpowder to rend asunder the aggregated atoms; no steam-engines to lift from their rocky beds the wrought columns of marble, tufa, syenite, etc., and send them forward to their distant temples and palaces. Did they possess mechanical arts and contrivances unknown to us, which rendered those great labors easy and of speedy accomplishment? We think not. The ancients depended upon *brute force*, upon *numbers*, to carry forward their vast undertakings. The element of *time* hardly entered into their calculations. Time and human life were not held in very high regard in the old heathen world. They accomplished by slow, tedious, and imperfect processes, what we do rapidly and perfectly by the aid of science, skill, and the most suitable machinery and tools. The fluting of their columns, the elaborate working of their bas-reliefs, friezes, entablatures, etc., were done by the slow picking and chiselling of many imperfect tools in many hands. The raising of a block of marble was accomplished by direct human strength, which was secured by the aid of many strong muscles.

In the time of the Roman emperors, the whole known world was *owned* by about *thirty thousand* men. These rich nobles and patricians held as slaves all the rest of mankind, and could command their services. In great works, like those upon which we employ a thousand workmen, they would employ a hundred thousand, and thus, through force of numbers, compensate in some degree for our superior mechanical appliances and intelligent skill.

No structures ever erected by human hands have excited so much wonder as the pyramids of Egypt. According to Herodotus, one hundred thousand men worked forty years in constructing that of Cheops. It rises into the air four hundred and fifty-two feet, and covers a square whose side is seven hundred and sixty-eight feet, and is built of vast blocks of stone, brought from quarries many miles distant. We are entirely ignorant regarding the means employed to transport and raise these stones to their resting-places. It is not probable, however, that any art or mechanical contrivance superior, or in any respect equal, to those known to us was brought into requisition. It has been estimated that ten thousand men, in our age, with our machinery, would raise a structure equally vast and imposing in less than fifteen years.

The subject upon which we have entered, to be treated in a satisfactory manner, requires much more space than the limits of this essay afford. The design has been, merely to give some brief reasons for dissenting from the popular idea that the ancients were acquainted with many arts and processes of superior merit which have been quite lost to us.

THE HUMAN HAIR.

THE deep interest felt in the welfare of the natural covering to the head is evinced by the expenditure of much time and large sums of money by all classes of people in attempting to preserve and adorn it. Upon no subject have we been more frequently requested to express opinions or supply information than upon that of the hair, and the increasing demand for dyes, washes, and "preservatives" indicates how wide-spread and well-nigh universal is the interest in the matter. These considerations have led us to make some observations upon the hair, and the substances used to change its tints and improve its condition.

The adornment of the hair, and the forming of it into fantastic shapes, have been practised by women in all ages, and in no direction have the caprices of fashion been more strikingly displayed than in disposing this natural covering of the head. The early Hebrew women gloried in their luxuriant tresses, plaiting them, and adorning their heads with ornaments of gold, silver, and precious stones. The Greeks allowed their hair to grow to a great length, while the Egyptians often removed it as an incumbrance. There is no "fashion" connected with the hair, in vogue at the present time, which is new. It is not a modern idea to resort to borrowed or "false" hair to satisfy the caprice of fashion, neither is it to dye the hair, or dress it with unguents and oily substances.

The Greek, Egyptian, Carthaginian, and Roman ladies, more than twenty-five centuries ago, made use of the most extravagant quantities of borrowed hair, and they wound it into large protuberances upon the back of their heads, and to keep it in place used "hair-pins" of precisely the form in use at the present time. The Roman women of the time of Augustus were especially pleased when they could outdo their rivals in piling upon their heads the highest tower of borrowed locks. They also arranged rows of curls formally around the sides of the head, and often the very fashionable damsels would have pendent curls in addition. An extensive commerce was carried on in hair, and after the conquest of Gaul, blonde hair, such as was grown upon the heads of German girls, became fashionable at Rome, and many a poor child of the forests upon the banks of the Rhine parted with her locks to adorn the wives and daughters of the proud conquerors. The great Cæsar indeed, in a most cruel manner, cut off the hair of the vanquished Gauls, and sent it to the Roman market for sale, and the cropped head was regarded in the conquered provinces as a badge of slavery.

To such a pitch of absurd extravagance did the Roman ladies at one time carry the business of adorning the hair, that upon the introduction of Christianity, in the first and second centuries, the apostles and fathers of the church launched severe invectives against the vanity and frivolity of the practice. It must be confessed the ancient ladies did outdo their modern sisters. The artistic, professional hair-dressers of old Rome were employed at exorbitant prices to form the hair into fanciful devices, such as harps, diadems, wreaths, emblems of public temples and conquered cities, or to plait it into an incredible number of tresses, which were often lengthened by ribbons so as to reach to the feet, and loaded with pearls and clasps of gold. No wonder such exhibitions of vanity excited the wrath of that stubborn old bachelor, St. Paul, and called forth his maledictions. It would be curious if, before the present fashion of arranging the hair among the ladies runs out, the extreme customs of a pagan age should come round again.

In ancient times people grew old as they do now, and the frosts of age blanched the raven locks of youth, and also there were those with hair glowing with red, or other tints not deemed desirable.

Hence it was that hair-dyes came into use; and a brisk demand for substances capable of changing the color of the hair has been maintained for thirty centuries.

The substances employed before the science of chemistry was understood were usually quite ineffectual in their influence. They were, for the most part, fugitive vegetable stains, which water would easily remove. There was, however, a metallic mixture made in Egypt which possessed qualities of the highest excellence. If the statements of some writers can be relied upon, this mixture was far superior to any form of hair-dye known to modern chemists. There is at the present time a dye used by the Armenians, in the East, which may be, in many respects, like the ancient dye. It is a metallic substance, resembling dross. This is powdered, and mixed with fine nut-galls, and moistened. A little of the paste is taken in the hand and rubbed into the hair or beard, and in a few days it becomes beautifully black. Those who have visited the Armenian convents in Turkey must have admired the fine black beards of the monks, even those of advanced age. This dye is undoubtedly composed of a mixture of iron and copper, which metals, in conjunction with the gallic acid formed from the galls, produce a dye of superior excellence.

The hair-dyes in use at the present time are, for the most part, objectionable in some one of the features, or they are untidy or inconvenient to apply. The dye which has been so fashionable during the past ten years is a poisonous compound, being composed largely of one of the salts of lead, — the acetate. This mixture was brought into notice soon after the close of the Mexican War, and was known as "General Twiggs's Hair-dye," from the name of the person who first successfully used it. Nearly all the "Restoratives," "Washes," "Embrocations," "Dressings," "Dyes," etc., found in the shops are identical in composition, being made from this formula. The number of popular mixtures of this kind, having different names, and which were made and sold by different parties, at one time exceeded *forty* in the United States. The formula and method of preparing it are exceedingly simple. Take of—

>Finely powdered acetate of lead, 120 grains.
>Lac sulphur, 160 grains.
>Rose-water, one pint.
>Glycerine, one ounce.

Mix the glycerine with the water, and add the acetate of lead and sulphur. The mixture must be well shaken before using. The lead and sulphur do not all dissolve in the rose-water, but fall to the bottom of the vessel as a precipitate. This preparation will gradually dye the hair a black or dark brown color, if a small quantity is rubbed into it once or twice a day. Its frequent use is however attended with great danger, as numerous instances of lead poisoning have resulted from its employment. There are many other hair-dyes into which lead enters that are equally objectionable. The following is a well known formula: —

>Powdered litharge (oxide of lead), 2 oz.
>Quicklime, ½ oz.
>Calcined magnesia, ½ oz.

Mix the powders, moisten with water, apply the paste to the hair, and allow it to remain four hours. This affords a dark brown color; for a deep black, it must remain eight hours.

The solution of plumbate of potash is a very convenient dye. It is slow in its action, but it does not stain the skin. It is prepared by dissolving in four ounces of liquor potassæ as much freshly precipitated oxide of lead as it will take up, and diluting the clear solution with twelve ounces of pure water. It may be applied as a wash to the hair. The permanganate of potassa forms an excellent dye, where a dark brown color is desired. It is safe and easily applied, but it has the disadvantage of staining the skin. If care is used, this need not occur. The solution may be made by dissolving in two ounces of distilled water 120 grains of the crystals of permanganate of potassa.

One of the most common forms of hair-dye, as found in the shops, is prepared from nitrate of silver, as follows: —

> Nitrate of silver, 1 oz.
> Rose-water, 7 oz.
> Dissolve the nitrate in the rose-water.

This is the dye. Previous to applying it, the hair must be wet with the following solution: —

> Sulphuret of potassium, 1 oz.
> Water, 6 oz.

After the hair is dry, the silver solution is applied with a brush. The odor of the mordant is very disagreeable; and this dye, although very quick and certain in action, cannot be regarded as very desirable. An inodorous silver dye is prepared as follows: Dissolve one ounce of nitrate of silver in six ounces of water, then add liquid ammonia by degrees, until the solution becomes cloudy from the formation of oxide of silver; continue to add ammonia until it becomes clear again from the redissolving of the oxide of silver. This is the dye. Before applying it, the hair must be washed in a solution of pyrogallic acid, made by dissolving sixty grains of the acid in eight ounces of rose-water. This is an excellent and safe dye; but its employment is attended with some trouble, and care must be used. A large number of other formulas for hair-dyes might be given, but these are sufficient. Their nature and methods of use will be readily understood.

The frequent use of "oils," "bear's-grease," "arctusine," "pomades," "lustrals," "rosemary washes," etc., etc., upon the hair, is a practice not to be commended. All of these oils and greasy pomades are manufactured from lard-oil and simple lard. No "bear's-grease" is ever used. If it could be procured readily, it should not be applied to the hair, as it is the most rank and filthy of all the animal fats. There are many persons whose hair is naturally dry and crisp, and in most families there is a want of some innocent and agreeable wash or dressing which may be used moderately and judiciously. The mixture which may be regarded as the most agreeable, cleanly, and safe, is composed of cologne spirit and pure castor-oil. The following is a good formula: —

> Pure, fresh castor-oil, 2 oz.
> Cologne spirit (95 per cent.), 16 oz.

The oil is freely dissolved in the spirit, and the solution is clear and beautiful. It may be perfumed in any way to suit the fancy of the purchaser. The oil of the castor-bean has for many years been employed to dress the hair, among both savage and civilized nations, and it possesses properties which admirably adapt it to this use. It does not rapidly dry, and no gummy, offensive residuum remains after taking on the chemical changes which occur in all oils upon exposure to light and air. It is best diffused by the agency of strong spirit, in which it dissolves. The alcohol or spirit rapidly evaporates, and does not in the slightest degree injure the texture of the hair. This preparation, for dressing the hair of children or ladies, will meet nearly or quite all requirements. A cheap and very good dressing is made by dissolving four ounces of perfectly pure, dense glycerine in twelve ounces of rose-water. Glycerine evaporates only at high temperatures, and therefore under its influence the hair is retained in a moist condition for a long time. As a class, the vegetable oils are better for the hair than animal oils. They do not become rancid and offensive so readily, and they are subject to different and less objectionable chemical changes. Olive-oil and that derived from the cocoa-nut have been largely employed, but they are inferior in every respect to that from the castor-bean.

It is doubtful if any mixture or substance has ever been devised which will restore hair to a bald head. A great many washes and embrocations are manufactured, all of which usually fail to meet the end desired. The falling of the hair is the result of diseased action in the hair follicles, or of a morbid condition of the entire scalp. When a hair is pulled out by its "roots," its base exhibits a bulbous enlargement of which the exterior is tolerably firm, while its interior is occupied by a softer substance which is known as the "pulp;" and it is to the continued augmentation of this pulp in the deepest part of the follicle, and to its conversion into the peculiar substance of the hair when it has been pushed upwards to its narrow neck, that the *growth* of the hair is due. A hair does not begin to grow from the true skin, but originates in the *epidermis*, and is essentially like that covering, being composed of aggregations of cells filled with horny matter, and frequently much altered in form. Hence it will be understood how difficult it is to excite action in a part possessed of such low vitality, and how poor the prospect must be of compelling hair to grow by any stimulus externally applied. Still, mixtures containing ammonia, vinegar, soap, and vesicating tinctures are sometimes thought to prove beneficial. The fall of the hair will usually cease from natural causes in a short time, the germinal vessels taking on healthy action spontaneously. The frequent washing of the head in tepid or cold water, and friction with a brush or coarse towel, are to be commended.

MICHAEL FARADAY.

IT is interesting to learn some of the incidents in the life of Michael Faraday, the great chemist, who died in London a few years since. His parentage, birth, and early life afford so much encouragement to the indigent, obscure, but resolute, industrious youth of our country, that these incidents should be widely published. His origin is but a counterpart of that of his distinguished friend and patron, Sir Humphry Davy. In carefully studying the lives of all the great men through whose labors chemistry has been wrested from the hands of the superstitious and empirical, we are surprised to find that nearly all started in life without means, without education, without friends. Poor, obscure boys were they all, but possessed of a natural enthusiasm and love for science, and also an indomitable courage and perseverance. Who, that might have chanced to see that ungainly boy, with strange contortions of countenance, hanging on the doorgate of Mr. Borlase's house in Cornwall, would have ventured to predict the future eminence and renown of the man? When Mr. Davies Giddy

Gilbert took the hand of the poor boy, and asked who he was, he was told that he was "a son of Davy, the carver, and very fond of making chemical experiments." "Indeed, and is that all he has to recommend him?" A lad "wasting his time in foolish chemical experiments," up in the garret of Mr. Borlase, the surgeon-apothecary, to whom he was apprenticed, instead of compounding medicines in the shop below, would hardly attract patronage among the influential and the wealthy. But Mr. Gilbert befriended him, and had the high satisfaction of feeling, in later life, that he was the early benefactor of Sir Humphry Davy.

Davy, in turn, became the early friend and patron of the unknown and struggling boy, Faraday. He was born in London, September 22, 1791, and was the son of a poor blacksmith. His education, if it may be called such, was of the most rudimentary description. He was sent to a common day-school, and picked up some knowledge of reading, writing, and arithmetic. The common day-schools in England, at the present time, are poor enough; but in those days the teachers and the schools were very inferior and superficial; and so young Faraday must have graduated with but a slender stock of erudition. At thirteen, he was apprenticed to Mr. Riebau, a bookbinder in Blanford Street. It was during his apprenticeship that his mind took a decided bent towards scientific knowledge; and he spent all his intervals of leisure, and all his slender store of pocket money, in buying books and apparatus necessary for the investigation of natural science. He succeeded in raising money enough to purchase a book upon electricity, and from this learned how to construct an electrical machine. This he did from a common glass vial, using the roughest and crudest materials in the various parts; but he had the proud satisfaction of obtaining the "spark" upon the first trial. This success made him more ambitious; and he constructed another, with a proper cylinder, and of considerable power, and presently his humble room began to be embellished with quite a variety of apparatus; and, before his master was aware of what was occurring, his apprentice became the proud possessor of all the knowledge then before the world relative to electrical force.

Boys of this character, in no age of the world, have long remained in obscurity. When once the foot has rested upon the portals of the temple of science, the doors are opened in some mysterious way, so that the enthusiastic worshipper may enter at his will. A Mr. Dance observed what young Faraday was doing, and obtained permission for him to attend four lectures by Sir Humphry Davy, in the Royal Institution. This was the first great event in his career, and from it must be dated all his subsequent advancement and prosperity. In 1829, Dr. Paris wrote a note to Faraday, asking him for a statement of the circumstances by which he became connected with the Royal Institution. He returned the following charming autobiographical letter:—

To J. A. PARIS, M. D.

ROYAL INSTITUTION, *Dec.* 23, 1829.

MY DEAR SIR,— You asked me to give you an account of my first introduction to Sir Humphry Davy, which I am very happy to do, as I think the circumstances will bear testimony to his goodness of heart.

When I was a bookseller's apprentice, I was very fond of experiments, and very averse to trade. It happened that a gentleman, a member of the Royal Institution, took me to hear some of Sir H. Davy's last lectures in Albermarle Street. I took notes, and afterwards wrote them out more fairly in a quarto volume. My desire to escape from trade, which I thought vicious and selfish, and to enter into the service of science, which I imagined made its pursuers amiable and liberal, induced me at last to take the bold and simple step of writing to Sir H. Davy, expressing my wishes, and a hope that if an opportunity came in his way, he would forward my views. At the same time, I sent the notes I had taken at his lectures.

The answer, which makes all the point of my communication, I send you in the original, requesting you to take great care of it, and to let me have it back; for you may imagine how much I value it.

You will observe that this took place at the end of the year 1812; and early in 1813 he requested to see me, and told me of the situation of assistant in the laboratory of the Royal Institution, then just vacant.

At the same time that he thus gratified my desires as to scientific employment, he still advised me not to give up the prospects I had before me; telling me that science was a harsh mistress, and in a pecuniary point of view but poorly rewarding those who devoted themselves to her service. He smiled at my notion of the superior moral feelings of philosophic men, and said he would leave the experience of a few years to set me right on that matter.

Finally, through his good efforts, I went to the Royal Institution early in March of 1813, as assistant in the laboratory; and in October of the same year, went with him abroad as his assistant in experiments and in writing. I returned with him in April, 1813, resumed my station in the Royal Institution, and have, as you know, ever since remained there.

I am, dear sir, very truly yours,

M. FARADAY.

The following is the note of Sir Humphry Davy alluded to in Faraday's letter: —

TO MR. FARADAY.

SIR, — I am far from displeased with the proof you have given me of your confidence, and which displays great zeal, power of memory, and attention. I am obliged to go out of town, and shall not be settled in town till the end of January. I will then see you at any time you wish.

It would gratify me to be of any service to you. I wish it may be in my power. I am, sir, your obedient humble servant,

H. DAVY.

By apparently a short step, the quondam bookbinder's apprentice had now become an apprentice to science, and was favored with the friendship of one of her most distinguished votaries. At this stage, it may be well to glance backwards, and contemplate for a moment the true position of chemical science at this time. Although but little more than half a century has elapsed, it will be seen that this was before the discovery of many of the metals, and consequently before much progress was made in the arts. It was also before the discovery of electro-magnetism. In short, chemistry, at this date, had few claims to be called a science. What a rich field for discovery was open to the young experimenter, and how well he improved it! His first published researches were upon the relations between electricity and magnetism,—a subject of uncommon interest in 1820, as Oersted had that year made known his great discovery of electro-magnetism. He published a paper entitled "New Electro-Magnetic Motions," and another, "A Theory of Magnetism," in 1821. In 1823, appeared his paper "On the Condensation of Muriatic Acid into the Liquid Form." It was, however, by his "Researches in Electricity" that he won his greatest fame. He commenced the publication of these treatises in 1831, and continued them for a period of nearly thirty years, publishing one or two each year. Some of the most important discoveries are contained in these papers, and show him to have been one of the greatest investigators of natural laws the world has ever seen.

How strange must Faraday's eventful life have seemed to him in his later years! Starting from poverty and obscurity, without the education which the schools confer, he was, during the period of a full half-century, the companion of the learned and the great, who sought his acquaintance from all parts of the civilized world. The late Prince Albert loved to steal away from the vexations and cares of state, and hold, in Faraday's study, familiar conversations upon matters of science with this venerable man. He was always simple, sincere, unostentatious. He had no hankerings for places and honors. Such, in brief, was the career of Faraday, the blacksmith's son; and such may be the history of many of the youth who may read these pages. Chemistry in our country, in its industrial applications, opens a wide field for intelligent research; and the honors to be won are as accessible and numerous almost as they were fifty years ago, when Faraday left the shop of the bookbinder to experiment at the Royal Institution.

CHEMISTRY OF A LUMP OF SUGAR.

A REMARKABLE substance is found in the juices or sap of plants, which, when placed in the mouth, or brought in contact with the nerves of taste, produces a "sweet" sensation. This is sugar. It has been stated that the human organism is capable of producing sugar, and that it is secreted by the liver in considerable quantities. We believe that hepatic sugar is not produced directly by that organ, but that it secretes a substance which, on exposure to the air, changes to sugar instantly. Vegetables alone seem to be the main agencies for manufacturing this interesting and important substance. A lump of sugar is *sweet;* a lump of salt, *pungent,* or *bitter;* a lump of cream of tartar, *sour;* why this difference in substances so much alike physically? The substances are all colorless, resemble each other in crystalline structure, cohere together in a similar manner, and are about equally soluble in water. Chemistry reveals to us the simple fact that in the constitution of these bodies different elements are employed, and the grouping of the atoms varies considerably; and this is all the information it affords. How different nerve sensations are produced, neither chemistry nor any other science is capable of informing us.

Sugar, in its chemical constitution, presents many features so remarkable they cannot fail to attract the attention and excite interest in the mind of every intelligent reader. The most striking relate to its molecular construction, and the instability or antagonisms which exist among the atoms. An atom of sugar may be compared to the main-spring of a watch wound up to the highest point attainable. In this state it represents force under the restraint of agencies which it seeks constantly to overcome. The cog and balance wheels maintain the tension and hold it in place; the slightest slip or disarrangement in these, and the complication of wheels is set to whizzing, and the machinery soon runs down to an inactive, passive state. Thus it is with an atom of sugar. It is like a coiled spring, ready, from any slight disturbing cause, to run from its highly organized state down to dead, inorganic matter. Heat and acids disturb its molecular arrangement most readily, and form from it a variety of new substances. Place a little sugar upon a thin plate of metal, and hold it over the flame of an alcohol lamp; what a marvellous change occurs! The white crystalline substance begins to fuse, bubbles up, emits smoke and combustible gases; and finally, when the action subsides, there remains a black, crispy mass of charcoal, in every respect like that which results from the combustion of wood. From whence comes this charcoal? It is not derived from the air; it is not supplied from the heat. It exists in the sugar, and is only developed by the agency of heat. Paradoxical as it may seem, beautiful white sugar is largely made up of black carbon; but its color is hidden so that we cannot see it, and this brings us to consider the chemical nature of a lump of sugar. Sugar is a *ternary* compound; that is, one made up of three elements, — carbon, hydrogen, and oxygen. There are two prominent varieties, or kinds, which differ not in elementary constitution, but in the proportion of the atoms, or in the method of grouping the atoms: —

Cane sugar, or sucrose . . . $C_{12} H_{22} O_{11}$
Grape, or starch sugar, glucose . $C_6 H_{12} O_6$ (or $C_{12} H_{24} O_{12}$)

The difference between the sugars will be seen at once from a glance at the symbols and figures. Now this seems very slight, and yet they are quite dissimilar in effects. The two kinds mentioned are not the only ones known, as three or four others have been already distinctly pointed out. One kind of sugar abounds in the sugar-cane, in beet-roots, and parsnips; this is the sucrose. Another kind constitutes the sweet matter of many fruits, and may also be prepared by acting upon starch with acid; this is glucose. Another, which is known as levulose, or fruit sugar, is found, mixed with glucose, in honey and in manna, which is an exudation from a species of ash, *Fraxinus ornus*, common in southern Europe. Our meadow and upland grasses contain a sweet substance, which is probably cane sugar; and it is to this that much of the value of these plants as food for cattle may fairly be attributed. In the laboratory of the plant, cane sugar can be changed over into fruit or grape sugar, and back again, with apparently the greatest facility; but this we cannot do in our working laboratories. We can change cane to grape sugar; but we cannot move a step in the other direction. The chemist or discoverer who invents a way of changing grape sugar or starch sugar readily into sucrose or cane sugar will confer great benefit upon the arts, and immortality upon himself. It is doubtful if this will ever be accomplished. In all the chemical transformations involved in changing one sugar into another, no other elements but those of simple water are assimilated or used.

The sugar-cane furnishes immense quantities of sucrose; in fact, it stands first among the sources of supply, and beets come next. It is singular that a rank, reedy cane and a soft, pulpy root should supply sugar identical in composition, and in the largest quantities. Cane sugar is the sweetest of all the varieties, and it is distinguished for the readiness with which it crystallizes. The crystals are four-sided prisms, with rhomboidal bases, and are remarkably uniform in appearance. This is an article of luxury, rendered by habit almost a necessary of life to every class of the community, and it is consumed in vast quantities. Levulose or fruit sugar cannot be crystallized; it is a colorless syrup, nearly as sweet as cane sugar, and more soluble in water and alcohol than glucose. It is also more easily altered by heat or by acids; while, on the other hand, it is less readily acted upon by alkalies or ferments. Glucose is now manufactured in immense quantities in France, and to some extent in this country. It is recognized in commerce as a beautifully clear, heavy syrup, of a moderate sweetness, somewhat resembling glycerine, and is sold at a low price. It is used by confectioners, brewers, and distillers in their various manufactures and operations, but scarcely at all for domestic purposes. It is also undoubtedly used to adulterate the cheaper kinds of refined sugars, although the writer has never met with an instance of this kind of sophistication. It is made from potato starch, by the action of oil of vitriol or sulphuric acid. Thick, gelatinous starch is placed in a large clay or porcelain-lined vessel; dilute acid is added, and the mixture boiled for several hours.

The acid is then removed by chemical means, and the solution evaporated to a thick, heavy syrup; for the action of the acid upon the starch has converted it into sugar. Starch sugar and the sweet principle of grapes, when solidified, are regarded as identical. If we evaporate the starch syrup down to a point of great density, it will, in a few days, solidify into a mass of grape sugar, weighing more than the starch used in its manufacture. These are, indeed, curious transformations; but still more curious is the fact, that the acid undergoes no change whatever. It is all withdrawn in its original amount after the boiling is completed; nothing is absorbed from the air, and no other substances but dextrine or grape sugar generated. Our limits do not permit us to explain the nature of these wonderful chemical changes.

Allusion has been made to the instability of sugar as a chemical compound. The equilibrium of forces in such a body must be very different from that of an inorganic compound. It must be far weaker, and more subject to derangement. The elements are held together by a kind of balance of chemical attractions, and remain united only while that balance is exactly maintained. Sugar, even among organized bodies, is peculiarly weak and unstable in constitution. A rude diagram, after the following manner, will, perhaps, represent the nature of the antagonisms that exist in the atoms that constitute a lump of sugar:—

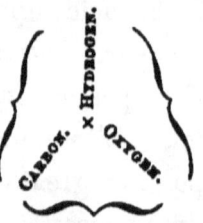

Here we have three of the most active of the elements, grouped in a way to produce a play of affinities, powerful and opposing. The oxygen and hydrogen tend, in the strongest manner, to unite and form water; they are prevented from doing so by the attraction of the carbon for both of them individually, while for their compound, water, that element has no apparent affinity whatever. The same is true of the other possible direct combinations. Carbon and hydrogen, carbon and oxygen, possess mutual attractive powers; but union between them is impossible, so long as the opposing force of the third element exists in sufficient intensity. These remarks and illustrations will serve to show how peculiarly organized is an atom of sugar, and what forces are pent up in the tiny grains.

The value of sugar depends upon its degree of sweetness; and as cane sugar excels in this particular, it is the most valuable. There is a popular notion that some pure sugars are sweeter than others, or "go farther," as the phrase is. This is an error. All specimens of cane sugar of equal purity are equally sweet. The apparent difference arises from physical causes, or from the different form and size of the crystals. The sensation of sweetness depends, in a measure, upon the rapidity with which the crystals dissolve in the mouth. Fine sugar is regarded as sweeter, because it dissolves faster than the large grained. A spoonful of the latter variety weighs less than the former, as the interstices between the grains are larger, and consequently the fine will sweeten a larger amount of liquid, because there is a larger amount of sugar in the spoon. As a general rule, it is poor economy to purchase impure sugars for household employment. In purchasing the damp, dark sugars of commerce, much moisture and molasses are bought at a high price; and although they seem sweeter and cheaper, such is not really the case. The process of refining is now carried to such perfection, and at so small expense, that the margin of cost between the pure and impure sugars is not worth considering.

The term "strong sugar" is often used by refiners, and has a meaning not well understood by grocers and consumers. The meaning is, not that one kind of rough sugar is sweeter than another, but that it has a better grain, and is therefore more profitable to manufacture. The refiner does not care so much about the color of the sugar he buys as he does about the distinctness of crystalline structure. The color he can remove; but if a large portion of the sugar is composed of molasses or uncrystallizable sugar, he is subjected to loss. Consumers of dark, coarse sugars are not generally aware of the fact that, beside the other impurities, they contain large numbers of a most disgusting insect —the *Acarus sacchari*. This insect is a very near relative of the *Acarus scabiei*, which produces the uncleanly and unpopular affection called the "itch." Indeed, the sugar insect often produces upon the hands and arms of grocers pustular eruptions, resembling true *psora*, or *scabies*. These insects burrow beneath the skin, and deposit their eggs, creating much irritation and an intolerable itching. The number of acari found in raw sugar is sometimes exceedingly great, and in no instance is the article entirely free from either the insects or their ova. Dr. Hassall examined one specimen, in which he estimated that no less than one hundred thousand existed in every pound of the sugar. In ten grains' weight he counted five hundred, many of which were so large as to be seen by the naked eye. He observes, that "it is inconceivable that thousands of these creatures can be introduced into the human stomach without serious endangerment to health;"

a suggestion which will naturally occur to the mind of every reader. The insect is never found in refined sugars.

In white candy or the finest loaf sugar we have the substance in a state of very high chemical purity, the only difference between them being the same as that seen on contrasting calcareous spar with white marble. The one exhibits large and distinct crystals; the other a confused assemblage of small ones. In manufacturing candy from molasses, an operation often performed in almost every household, the "candying" results from boiling the molasses to free it from water; and then, after cooling the waxy mass, pulling it by the hands, so as to develop the colorless saccharine crystals which serve to hide the dark impurities.

The sugar-refining process is exceedingly simple in all its details, and yet it requires the utmost care and experience. The raw sugar is dissolved in water, and mixed with albumen (white of eggs), serum of blood, or their equivalent, and the whole is heated to the boiling point. By the coagulation of the albumen the mechanical impurities are separated and removed. The syrup is then whitened or decolorized by filtering it through a bed of coarsely-powdered animal charcoal. This has the singular property of absorbing various organic coloring matters, so that the syrup comes through perfectly colorless.

It is then placed in " vacuum pans," and boiled, at a low temperature, until crystallization commences, or is effected; and pure white sugar is secured by placing the crystals in drying-rooms heated by steam.

It is quite impossible, in a paper necessarily so brief as this, to touch upon very many important points connected with the chemistry of sugar. Perhaps at another time the subject may be resumed, and a larger number of interesting facts presented.

FARM EXPERIMENTS AT LAKESIDE.

IN commencing a series of farm experiments in 1863, with the view of deciding some controverted points of much importance to the interests of husbandry, it was felt that no satisfactory results could be reached in less period of time than four or five years. The matter of *time* in all farm experiments, in my view, was of the highest importance, and therefore it was resolved to make no extended statements, and venture upon no conclusions, until the experiments had been carried through several successive seasons.

So far as I could learn, there were some interesting problems in agriculture which had never been satisfactorily solved in New England, or, in fact, in any section of our country. It seemed desirable to ascertain, approximately at least, by careful and extended experiment, the value of special or chemical fertilizing agents upon our New England soils, and in order to test this matter satisfactorily, it was clear that the experiments must be conducted upon a scale of considerable magnitude. If it was proved that a neglected, exhausted farm, embracing a variety of soils, with uplands and lowlands, could be brought into fair tilth by the use of special agents, it would serve as an important fact in the history of our agricultural industry; and further, if it could be done at a cost which would prove it to be practicable and remunerative, certainly great service would be conferred upon our farming interests.

The "Lakeside" farm, of about one hundred acres, which I purchased seven years since, was not what might be considered a worthless or barren tract; for some portions of it, a quarter of a century ago, were probably in fair condition, producing crops of hay and grain corresponding with those grown by the farmers of that period. For a long time, however, it had been in the hands of those who treated it with neglect, and the best fields had hardly been turned over with a plough, or cheered with a dressing of manure, for a score of years. It had therefore become in a great measure exhausted, and the thin grasses were suffering for aliment. The number of acres not devoted to wood and pasturing was about twenty-five; of this, nearly one half was a low, boggy meadow, upon which water was allowed to rest until it was removed by evaporation late in the spring. The remainder consisted of a series of elevations or hills of considerable altitude, dry and silicious upon the tops, but moist at the bases from retained water and from springs. The soil of the different fields afforded quite a vari-

FARM EXPERIMENTS AT LAKESIDE. 103

ety in character and composition, and probably as fairly represented the varying nature of our Massachusetts farms as any tract of land in the State. A portion was silicious, loose, and dry; another was loamy and retentive; another, moist and composed of dark mould with a clayey subsoil; and still another, a well-formed wet peat bog.

It will be seen from this brief description that the farm was made up of fields eminently suited for fair experiment, and also it will be understood that it came into my hands under the most favorable conditions to test the value of any plan or system of fertilization. In 1863, about ten tons of indifferent upland hay were cut upon the portion embraced in the original purchase; the produce of an adjoining field of four acres of upland, which has since been purchased and added to the farm, I am unable to state. No corn or other grain in any amount had been grown for perhaps ten years upon the farm, and I have no knowledge of the character of any cereals produced prior to the purchase. It should be stated here that the chemical analysis of soils taken from the different fields presented a singular difference in composition, and what I learned in this regard upon my own fields led me to examine those of others at comparatively remote points, and the same remarkable variations have been generally found to prevail. The soil at the base of a small hill or elevation is of a very different character from that at the apex, and a level flat at one extremity of a farm is quite unlike another at the opposite end. It is not necessary to leave our own farms to find soils presenting striking dissimilarities in chemical composition as well as in physical characteristics. This is a point which should receive more consideration in the conduct of our farms.

With the design of attempting to bring this farm into good condition without the use of barnyard or stable dung, no stock was kept upon the premises save a cow and a heifer the first two years, and with the exception of a few loads of manure purchased for garden uses at the start, no excrementitious products have been bought during the seven years it has been in my hands. The farm at the present time (1871) sustains eighteen cows, five horses, three hogs, and, for a portion of the year, one yoke of oxen. The product of hay in 1870 was fifty tons, corn two hundred bushels, rye perhaps twenty bushels, with large quantities of apples, grapes, and other fruits. The productive capabilities of the fields have been aroused through the agency of fertilizing substances outside of animal excrement, and the farm placed in position to maintain its good tilth by the manurial products which it is now capable of supplying. To state the matter explicitly, and thus avoid the possibility of any misunderstanding, the farm was raised from its unproductive condition, during the first three or five years of the experiment, by special fertilizers, so that by increase of products it has been made capable of sustaining a herd of animals, which animals now supply all the fertilizing material needed, and the manufacture and use of chemical fertilizers have been in a large measure suspended. In short, the experiment has practically come to an end through its perfect success.

In bringing about these results, fifteen tons of bones, one hundred bushels of unleached ashes, four tons of fish pomace, two tons of Peruvian guano, five hundred pounds of crude potash, one ton of oil of vitriol, ten casks of lime, and several hundred pounds altogether of sulphate of magnesia, nitrates of soda and potassa, chloride of sodium, oxide of manganese, sulphate of iron, sulphate of ammonia, etc., have been employed. Eight tons of the bones have been made on the farm into what is known as "superphosphate," by dissolving them in the condition of fine powder in oil of vitriol; three tons have been combined with unleached wood ashes; and the remaining four tons have been used in various ways, one portion in the raw or natural condition, another by rotting in contact with moist soil or peat, another for obtaining phosphoric acid, and in other forms for experimental purposes.

The other agents have been employed alone and in such combinations as were demanded to conduct the experiments understandingly, and in accordance with correct scientific deductions. It would require too much space to give a detailed account of these experiments; the statement presented is a general one, given for the purpose of affording a comprehensive idea of the extent and nature of the labors undertaken, and as preparatory to the presentation of the details of a few experiments of a more special character. During the past three years attention has been given to the production, saving, and application to the soil of animal excrements, and these observations ought not to pass unnoticed.

The cost of the bones and most of the other agents used upon the farm was less than they could be obtained for at the present time, as they were purchased during the years of great depression which existed in the time of the war. Twelve tons of raw, unground bones were purchased at the start, at a cost of only twelve dollars per ton. They were placed in a large steam-boiler, constructed of iron, and submitted to the action of high-pressure steam for a period of twelve hours. They were then removed, allowed to cool, and immediately reduced to powder by grinding in a machine resembling a common burr-mill. Bones by steaming are changed in their physical structure; the animal portion or the gelatine is in part removed, and the cell-structure, before tough and refractory, becomes brittle, and is readily broken up by grinding. After steaming, they can be ground in an ordinary plaster mill without obstructing the movements of the stones, and without requiring a greater expenditure of power than is needed to grind common gypsum. The only mill ever constructed, so far as I am informed, that will grind raw or unsteamed bones fine enough for agricultural uses, is what is known as the atmospheric centrifugal machine, which does its giant work by the single power of attrition. The fragments of bone are allowed to fall into a strong iron drum, which is made to revolve with immense velocity, and by the action of air, and of the fragments upon themselves, they are instantly reduced to an impalpable powder.

The rich nitrogenous principle of the bones used upon my farm, the gelatine, was secured and composted with dry peat and bone dust, and this was found to afford a most efficient top-dressing for grass lands. Thus, in the process of steaming nothing was lost. The cost of preparation was about equal to the original cost of the bones, and hence I have estimated it at twenty-five dollars the ton. The present market price of bone dust is sixty dollars the ton, which affords a wide margin between the expense of my bone material and that obtained through commercial channels.

The whole sum expended for special fertilizers during the past seven years is seven hundred and ninety dollars, or, in round numbers, eight hundred dollars, which, applied to twenty-five acres of land, gives as the cost of renovation about thirty-three dollars per acre. The price of fair stable manure in the city of Haverhill has, during the past seven years, ruled at about six dollars the cord. Add to this the cost of loading and hauling to the farm, about four dollars, and we have, as the entire cost of stable manure in the field, ten dollars the cord. Eight hundred dollars, the sum expended for special agents, would have provided me with about eighty cords of ordinary long manure. This would have given to each acre a little more than three cords; and now the question arises, Could the expenditure of eight hundred dollars for stable manure have secured fertilizing effects of equal value with those afforded by the plan of treatment pursued, costing the same? On the contrary, I am confident that to have started my farm and put my fields, by purchased manures, in the high tilth in which they are at present, would have cost perhaps double the sum which has been expended.

The amounts and cost statements presented are not exact, but sufficiently so to answer all the purposes of this discussion. Of course, in contrasting the cost of fertilizers, a great many little things should be taken into account. The difficulty and cost of placing bulky manure upon swampy lands and high elevations must not be overlooked, and the expense of handling or distributing it after it is deposited is considerable. Nearly one third of my tillage lands are so low that they cannot be entered upon by any vehicle drawn by oxen or horses, and consequently it is extremely difficult or well-nigh impossible to distribute heavy manures upon these fields. With the concentrated fertilizers employed, the men have been able to carry in a farm basket an amount of plant nutriment equal in value to that found in a cartload of animal excrement.

Upon the reclaimed meadows no farm dung has been used, excepting on a small patch for the purpose of experiment, and I have secured large crops of redtop and timothy during the past five years. The method of treatment has been varied, with the view of ascertaining the best way of bringing them into condition to produce upland grasses. I have dressed certain parcels with the farm-made superphosphate, with a mixture of bone and ashes, with guano, fish pomace, combinations of salt and lime, and with sulphate of ammonia and nitrate of soda. It must be remembered that my low lands are pure peat bogs, of such a nature that if the water was withdrawn, and the deposits allowed to become dry, fire would consume the whole to ashes. The elevation of the bog above the level of Lake Kenoza, upon which it borders, is only nine inches in the winter and spring, when the lake is at its highest altitude; consequently, it is an unpromising and difficult field upon which to experiment with the view of driving out worthless meadow grasses. Indeed, no one in whose judgment I placed confidence would afford me any encouragement to expect success. It was regarded as impossible to renovate meadows which for so large a part of the year were almost submerged, and which could not be drained. Nevertheless, the experiment has proved successful, and crops already secured have paid all the expenses of renovation and treatment. Upon two acres of the six which are now producing upland grasses, a coating of sand three inches in thickness was placed, after thoroughly spading and pulverizing the bog; upon this a dressing, made of equal parts of fine bone and ashes, two thousand pounds in quantity, was evenly distributed, and it was then seeded down with redtop and timothy, and covered in with a brush harrow. The work was done in the months of August and September, 1866. The first crop of hay in 1867 was a little more than one and a half tons to the acre, the succeeding crop was two and a half tons, and those which have since been taken from the field have averaged about the same amount. One acre of the remaining six received no coating of sand, but after digging out the hassocks and burning them, the patch was turned over with a spade, fertilized with three hundred pounds of bone dust and two hundred of guano, and seeded down like the other. This was accomplished in the autumn of 1868. In 1869 the first crop and aftermath gave three tons to the acre. In 1870 the two crops exceeded that amount. Another acre, bordering directly upon the lake, but slightly more elevated, was reclaimed in the same manner in 1867, and treated with one ton of dry fish pomace. It gave a crop the succeeding year of one and a half tons to the acre, and since then the yield has been about two tons each season. In 1869, two more acres were put in condition, fertilizing one half with pure bone and spent ashes, the other with farm superphosphate. The crop in 1870 upon both sections was nearly alike, slightly exceeding one and a half tons to the acre. Some of these experiments have been continued long enough to learn something of the value of the methods of treatment, while the others have not. Several plats of the meadow have been put in condition, and left one season without any fertilizing agents, and the result has been that ferns and coarse meadow plants have flourished together in rank luxuriance, thus proving the needed presence and high utility of the plant stimulants employed.

From the brief and imperfect statements presented, it will be conceded that wet peat meadows can be profitably reclaimed and fertilized by special or concentrated agents, easy and convenient to handle. I shall not venture upon the expression of opinions at present regarding the most effective and cheapest agents, as these points are not satisfactorily settled. After a few more seasons have passed, the results will enable me to form a more exact and reliable judgment in regard to the matter. The great value of our low lands is as yet imperfectly understood, although attention has been called to them persistently through books and the agricultural press. Farmers, as a general rule, fear to have anything to do with the soft peat bogs so common throughout the State. Their experience in miring oxen and horses in attempts to plough or haul on manure is not favorable to the prosecution of the work of renovation. When it is known that the spade will do the work of the plough, and that fertilizers of great efficiency can be carried in a basket upon the shoulder, a little more courage may possibly be infused into the owners of such lands, and they may seek to draw from them their hidden wealth by the work of reclamation. It must, however, be distinctly understood, that all meadows are not of a character to pay for any labor that may be bestowed upon them.

It is important that every farmer should carefully examine his low grounds before commencing improvements, that he may not subject himself to disappointment and loss. It is certainly difficult clearly to describe a meadow which will not, after working, bear good crops of sweet grasses, but I am confident I could point out such, if allowed five minutes' work upon it with a spade. A piece of low land deficient in peat, with a superficial clayey covering, overrun with moss or short, matted grass, will not pay for the labor of renovation; neither will a meadow pay if it is surrounded with a forest which places it in shade half the hours of the day, no matter what may be the nature of the deposit. A meadow permanently wet, and which cannot be drained, is one upon which labor is usually wholly lost. Any low land open to the air and sunlight, which has a good bottom of peat or black mould, and is raised one foot above the highest water level in the spring, can be converted into a profitable field, yielding abundance of the nutritious grasses. More attention should be bestowed upon such lands, as the hay crop is one of the most important and profitable produced upon our farms.

A series of extended and systematic experiments have been undertaken upon the farm in connection with fields which are elevated and dry, and which were unproductive at the time they were commenced. A measured acre of land of this nature was ploughed in the autumn of 1863, and in the succeeding spring dressed with five hundred pounds of pure, fine bone, sown broadcast, and then planted with corn, a handful of farm-made superphosphate being placed in each hill. One hundred and fifty-seven bushels of corn in the ear were taken from the field in the autumn of 1864. After the corn was removed the land was ploughed, and again dressed with eight hundred pounds of a mixture consisting of ashes, bone dust, and refuse saltpetre, and sowed down to winter rye and seeded with timothy. The crop was thirty-one bushels of nice, plump grain. The season of 1866 was exceedingly dry, and the tender grass roots were so parched with heat, that the hay crop was cut short materially. The product of this field was only twenty-three hundred pounds. The next season a top-dressing was given it of five hundred pounds of a compost of gelatine and peat (the gelatine being the liquid or resultant product coming from the steaming of bones), and the hay crop reached forty-three hundred pounds. The crop of 1868, with the aftermath, reached two and a half tons. That of 1869, after a top-dressing of two hundred pounds of Peruvian guano, was two and a quarter tons. In 1870 it was a little less than two tons. In this experiment, a dry field, originally exhausted, has been treated exclusively with concentrated fertilizers, and carried over a period of seven years, the seasons embracing the extremes of dry and wet, and these are the results. Are they satisfactory, or is the experiment a successful one?

The corn crop, seventy-eight bushels of shelled corn to the acre, is not bad; the rye crop, thirty-one bushels, would not be disappointing to most farmers; and the succeeding crops of hay, amounting in the five consecutive years to nearly ten tons, are certainly a fair product for high land, subject to unfavorable influence of drought. The cash value of the crops at the farm, if they had been sold at the time they were gathered, would have reached fully four hundred dollars the acre. But it should be stated that corn in 1864 was worth two dollars and fifty cents the bushel, and all the crops have ruled high since. The cost of the fertilizing agents employed has been a little over forty-four dollars; the cost of labor cannot be exactly stated, but it is certain the field has afforded a clean profit of one hundred per cent. each year.

If space permitted, the details of other experiments undertaken on the farm might be given, but enough has been said to convey a general idea of the nature and design of the work. It is worth something to know that a run-down farm can be in a fair measure rejuvenated and made productive by a class of manurial agents which do not partake of the nature of animal excrement. It is worth much to know that these agents are proved capable of exerting a *sustaining* influence upon our soils, that these fertilizing effects are felt year after year, and that crops do not rapidly falter when they can draw nutriment from no other sources. We have learned that remunerative crop returns are possible and probable when special fertilizing agents are employed in their highest integrity, and when a fair profit only is paid in the purchase of the raw materials. Before passing to the consideration of another topic incident to this discussion, I will briefly allude to the grain crops produced upon the farm.

A crop of corn has been raised each season since 1864, and also a crop of spring wheat until the present year. Rye, oats, roots, and potatoes, with the various grasses, complete the list. From careful records of expenses and results, the corn crop is found to have been the most remunerative, and the wheat comes next. During the seven consecutive seasons closing in 1870, we have passed through great vicissitudes of meteorological changes: we have had seasons characterized by extreme wet, and by unparalleled heat and drought; some have been quite extended, and others have been very brief. That of 1869 gave us only about one hundred days in which to plant and harvest our corn; that of 1870 was of extraordinary length, the warm growing weather lasting from early in April to November. It has been a period of great value to those who wish to gain by experiment and observation a knowledge of the best methods of farming under the extremes of heat and cold, wet and dry, and of the crops best suited to our capricious climate. The farmer who, by imperfect tillage and lazy habits, has reached the conclusion that we in New England have no certain crops, is indulging in grievous error. All our cereal and grass crops are certain enough if our fields are in perfect condition, but corn may be said never to fail if a reasonable amount of attention is given it. My crop has never fallen below seventy bushels of shelled corn to the acre, and in 1869 I grew, in about one hundred days, a crop of *one hundred and six bushels to the acre.* So late was this season that on the 10th of April I was able to walk across the ice-bound lake upon which my fields border, and snow rested on my potato patch the 2d day of May. Corn, among crops with us in Massachusetts, is like a Bronsonian Democrat; it rises "superior to its accidents." The crop at Lakeside in 1870, hot and parched as the season was, reached seventy-five bushels to the acre. The cost of the corn in the aggregate, raised during the seven seasons, does not exceed forty-five cents per bushel. This estimate includes one half the cost of the fertilizers and all the labor from the time of planting to shelling, but it *does not* take into account the fodder, which has proved in my experience to have a high value. This has been fed to milch cows in association with wheat straw in the long and cut condition, and careful observation and experiment show that, as a milk-producing agent, it is worth nearly as much as upland hay. Corn is the cereal to which farmers should give special attention. To grow it profitably, we must grow *large quantities on small parcels of ground.* It requires no greater expense or labor to raise seventy-five to one hundred bushels to the acre, than to raise twenty-five. Corn can be grown in good quantity for several consecutive years upon the same field by the use of agents which hold those great essentials to plant-growth, — phosphoric acid, potash, and lime; but to attain to the highest success, substances capable of affording the nitrogenous element must be added. The first three years of my experiments with the corn crop, I depended solely upon dressings composed of lime, potash or ashes, and flour of bone, and my crops were excellent; but I now use in association four cords of good fresh farm dung to the acre, spread over the ploughed field, and harrowed in with a Geddes harrow. In the hills, at the time of planting, I place a handful of a mixture of fine bone and ashes, and under this treatment I have learned to anticipate heavy crops with full confidence. For corn, or indeed for any crop, I prefer to plough in the autumn. One of the most important items to be taken into account in the cultivation of the soil is the fineness of the mould in which the seed is placed. A hard, lumpy, imperfectly pulverized field, holding equal amounts of the elements of plant nutrition with one that is fine, will fall short usually twenty per cent. in product under the same meteorological conditions. In fall ploughing we secure the disintegrating influence of frost upon our furrows, and this is costless aid in soil cultivation.

For five consecutive years I have not failed, under what I regard as proper soil treatment, to secure good crops of wheat. In one season, that of 1867, it fell to twenty-one bushels to the acre, but the others have not gone below thirty. It was, indeed, singular to find what a strong prejudice existed among farmers against attempts to raise this noble grain. It was urged that it could not be grown on our soils, they were worn out, did not hold lime or something else necessary to its development; and further, if it did grow, rust, mildew, or insects would destroy the crop before maturity. The first year, I grew a crop of plump wheat, thirty-one bushels to the acre, while other farmers were growing barley, fifteen bushels to the acre. I sold my wheat at $3.50, while the barley went for $1.40 per bushel. The plan of soil treatment has been to sow broadcast early in the season five hundred pounds of farm superphosphate to the acre, mixed with one hundred pounds of crude nitrate of potassa, or one hundred and fifty pounds of nitrate of soda and fifty pounds of sulphate of magnesia. The importance of magnesia in the ash of wheat has been strangely overlooked by chemists and by experimenters, and I regard the employment of a salt holding this element, in dressings for wheat land, as of great utility. Nearly one eighth of the ash of wheat is made up of magnesia, and as our granite New England soils cannot well supply it, we must furnish it in our manures. As regards the evil influence of rust upon wheat, I am inclined to the opinion that a well-fed, vigorous plant possesses a power of resistance to parasitic growths, which is in a considerable degree protective. I do not mean to say that the farmer can positively and always place himself beyond the reach of disasters resulting from fungoid plants or destructive weather influences; but I do say, that a good, vigorous, well-fed stalk of wheat, corn, or other grain, will bear up under adverse influences better than one that is half starved and weakly. The battle is in favor of the strong and against the weak among plants, as well as among men and animals.

I regret that there are many perhaps well-meaning but poorly informed writers in our agricultural papers, and speakers at agricultural meetings, who make statements and give expression to views which tend directly to lead farmers astray, and to confuse and perplex them upon the subject of fertilizers, greatly to their detriment. And unfortunately these absurd and erroneous statements and strange exhibitions of selfishness connected with agricultural matters are not confined to those who are ignorant; we have had some sad examples from the opposite class. It is only about a year since that a gentleman intimately connected with the interests of agriculture delivered and published an address upon special fertilizers, in which he deliberately advises farmers to abstain from any attempts to prepare their own superphosphate, assuring them that they cannot successfully accomplish the work. In another part of the same address he informs them that he himself is engaged in the manufacture of superphosphate upon a large scale, and the inference is, that farmers should buy his *honest* products. As we looked through this address, or advertising circular, we could not help exclaiming, "Alas! upon whom can the farmer depend? If interest and avarice confront him, when moving within the circle of those who should be safe advisers and trusty friends, to whom can he flee for counsel and protection?"

It is not alone in regard to the nature and methods of making and applying fertilizers that farmers are led into error; but perhaps there is no subject upon which it is more important that correct knowledge should be disseminated than this. Some of the best known and most widely circulated of our agricultural journals have advised farmers to collect large quantities of bones, reduce them to fragments by pounding, and then dissolve them by pouring on sulphuric acid; and the same wise advice has been given at the meetings of Farmers' Clubs. Now, it would seem that every intelligent person ought to know that raw, unground bones *cannot* be dissolved in sulphuric acid. Whoever recommends this course, purposely misleads, or else is in ignorance from never having tried the experiment. Fragments no larger than a raisin may remain in strong or dilute acid for months, and not be perceptibly acted upon. They are attacked only upon the surface when in contact with oil of vitriol, and a film of insoluble sulphate of lime is formed which effectually arrests further action. In order to dissolve bones and fit them for plant nutriment, they must first be ground to fine powder, and the finer the better, as the acid can then cut through the little atoms and disintegrate the structure. We must not mislead or be misled in this matter. If a farmer has a quantity of raw bones which have been picked up, it is probable they cannot be ground in any mill within his reach, and he cannot dissolve them in acid. His best plan is to dissolve them by either packing in good wood ashes after the method which has been often described, and which I presume is well understood, or burn them to whiteness, and then have them ground in a plaster mill. Bones piled in a heap with wood, will ignite and burn with great fierceness. The calcined product is brittle and can easily be ground, and the powder, dissolved in acid, forms an excellent superphosphate.

It seems to be necessary to state again and again, that in order to obtain from bones the full fertilizing influence they are capable of affording, they must be reduced to an impalpable powder, that it is a waste to sow upon fields bones which are simply crushed into fragments, so as to be seen readily by the eye. In 1864, I sowed upon a field a bushel of bone fragments, none of them larger than a pea or bean, and in the summer of 1870, upon turning over the field with the plough, they were brought to the surface entirely unchanged. Ordinary soil and atmospheric influences will not disintegrate and render available, as plant food, bones in the whole or crushed condition during the lifetime of any farmer, though he may live far beyond the common age of man. This important truth should be understood by all who desire to use bones in connection with their crops.

In the renovation of my farm by the employment of special fertilizers, I have kept a few prominent, well established facts and principles in view, and have never allowed myself to be diverted, turned aside, or confused by any apparently conflicting statements or alleged results on the part of others. A truth is a truth, a fact is a fact, no matter how difficult it may sometimes be to compel all agencies and influences to contribute to the establishment of verities. I believe we have some truths, some facts in agriculture; although the contrary view ought to prevail, if the contradictory opinions and statements of many of its professed friends are entitled to regard. Chemistry is an exact science; it is based on the retort, the balance, and mathematics; and when its aid is called in to inform us regarding the constitution of plant structures, its teachings are infallible. We can no more escape from its demonstrated facts in this department, than we can from a belief in those applied principles which enable us to produce, in our industrial laboratories, the wonderful and complex bodies which contribute so essentially to the welfare and comfort of the race. Chemistry has never rendered and never will render such aid to agriculture as will direct the farmer how to raise crops without the expenditure of time and labor, and the exercise of a reasonable amount of skill and common sense; but it does inform him precisely regarding the nature of the plant structures he is called upon to rear, and the food they demand, and this knowledge is of immense service. Chemistry, in its practical hints and teachings to agriculturists, leaves a void which must be filled up by inferences and by the exercise of the ingenuity and the judgment, and any farmer who is incapable of exercising these desirable faculties can never be greatly benefited in his labors by science.

The hinderances to success in the use of special fertilizing agents upon the farm are not numerous, but they are of a nature peculiarly provoking, and perhaps in some degree discouraging. The greatest of these are connected with the sources of supply, and it is in this direction that we must bend all our energies to bring about a salutary reform. I am free to say that in the farm experiments undertaken, an advantage has resulted from being able to secure and employ only such agents as were of absolute integrity, and also my professional pursuits naturally tend to afford a facility and accuracy of manipulation which can hardly be expected of most of those in the pursuits of husbandry. Still, the great obstacle to success in the use of special fertilizers lies in their sophistication and general worthlessness. It is not alone in the so-called "superphosphate" that frauds are practised, but there are deceptions, attenuations, and admixtures in connection with almost all agents which science and experience have pointed out as sources of plant nutriment. A certain class of substances, which have hitherto passed almost unsuspected and unchallenged through the channels of trade, can manifestly no longer remain above suspicion. Unleached wood ashes, when pure, are of the highest service to farmers and gardeners, and they are diligently sought for by almost every one who has lands to till. Specimens of dry ashes, sold as those of wood, have been brought to me, which upon chemical examination were found to be composed of more than fifty per cent. of coal ashes. A schooner-load of ashes brought from an Eastern port, and purchased by a friend at twenty-five cents a bushel, proved to have only an actual value of five cents a bushel. Analysis of a specimen of these ashes was made, with a view of purchasing a quantity if they proved satisfactory. The examination gave the following result: —

Hydrate of lime	55 parts.
Silica	13 "
Charcoal	7 "
Ashes, mixture of wood and coal	25 "
	100 parts.

The large percentage of lime is due to the fact that the ashes came from a limestone district, and were probably taken from lime-kilns.

Another substance known as "fish guano" or "fish pomace" has acquired considerable reputation in this section as a fertilizing agent, especially for grass lands. It consists of the dry residuum of the fish-oil factories on the New England coast, and is made up of the crushed bones and integuments of fishes, from which the oil has been separated by great pressure. When pure and dry we have found it to be a good and convenient plant stimulant, and worth about twenty dollars a ton. Probably but few of those who have become purchasers of this substance have suspected that it is often so largely adulterated as to be comparatively worthless. Some specimens found in the market, and probably sold extensively to farmers, upon analysis gave the following results:—

Water	17.26
Sand	46.00
Phosphate of lime	8.90
Organic matter holding ammonia and salts of potash, soda, etc.	27.84
	100.00

Here we have *sixty-three* per cent. of *sand and water*, which are worthless materials, and which are paid for at the rate of twenty or twenty-five dollars a ton.

Another specimen gave: —

Water	31.00
Organic matter	35.00
Phosphate of lime and various salts with sand	34.00
	100.00

This is better, but still *one third* of the whole bulk is perfectly worthless. A popular "superphosphate," recently examined, gave twenty-two per cent. of water, and only five and one half per cent. of soluble phosphate. The fact that husbandmen are not generally competent to judge of the value of compounds offered as fertilizers, has led to placing on sale some of the most absurd substances and mixtures which human ingenuity can discover or devise.

A heavy powder called the "Grafton Mineral Fertilizer" has come into the market within a year or two, and has secured a large sale at high prices. What is the nature of this powder? Let us judge of it by the analysis which is presented in connection with its sale. Here it is: —

Silica	30.3
Protoxide of iron	6.27
Lime	20.6
Magnesia	11.17
Carbonic acid	32.11

This statement gives 30 per cent. sand, a small quantity of iron, and the remainder is carbonate of lime and magnesia. One third (the sand), it is plain to see, is worthless; the iron is of no account, as every soil in New England furnishes from the decomposition of the sulphurets an abundant supply; the carbonates of lime and magnesia are worth something, but how much? little more than ground oyster or clam shells. As a fertilizing substance it manifestly has no great value.

A concentrated liquid fertilizer, put up in stone jugs, each holding a quart, for which the modest sum of two dollars and fifty cents is charged, has been, I am informed, largely sold in many sections of the country. This is a palpable fraud which needs no comment.

In view of what we know of the nature of commercial fertilizing agents, is it necessary to inquire why so small an amount of benefit is received from the application of these substances to our lands? When a farmer purchases and employs, in connection with his crops, fertilizers of unknown value, of what value are his experiments to himself or anybody else? If he fails of satisfactory results, upon what or upon whom can he lay the blame? If he secures a successful crop, does he know whether it is due to the fertilizer or to a favorable season, or to good culture, or to some other agency? He certainly can form no satisfactory opinion upon the subject.

How can this evil be met and overcome? Legislation has thus far failed to afford a remedy, and it is extremely difficult to circumvent human selfishness and ingenuity by statute laws. There are only two ways: one is to have all fertilizing agents of home production, of domestic manufacture; the other is, to form associations among farmers, establish factories, and prepare the agents only for use among those who are interested in their production. The motive of gain must be taken away or removed in some way, before the valuable plant stimulants will come into our hands in such a condition that they can be employed with confidence and success.

Stable dung is sold upon an improper or wrong basis, the price being fixed on bulk with little or no reference to quality. Now, we know that the stable manure from one cellar or vault may be, and often is, worth double that taken from another. A man who feeds his horse or other animals upon run hay, and stints the use of grain, supplies to the purchaser or user a very poor article of excrement; and in livery stables the straw and litter serve to give great bulk, but little weight or substance, to the product of the yard or vault. I have ascertained by experiment, that excrementitious manures, as produced at my farm, held of fertilizing substances nearly two and a half times as much in the cord as was found in those obtained from stable vaults in the city.

It is of the highest consequence in successful farming that the actual quality of fertilizing agents be considered, rather than appearances, bulk, or color. Every substance that holds potash, phosphoric acid, lime, soda, and the nitrogenous bodies, has *value*, and the value depends upon the amount and the condition in which these agents exist in the substance. If we can know what is the exact value of the agent we are using, we can experiment understandingly and successfully; but if we are at work in the dark, our results will be wholly unreliable and valueless.

The results of our experiments have established this point clearly, that in order to grow crops successfully, *all* the substances needed by plants must be present in the soil in which they flourish. The soils of cultivable lands hold in a greater or less proportion all that is essential to the growth of plants. Sometimes one or more of these essentials is largely in excess, or there is more than is needed by any crop for a succession of years; and often one or more are held in small amount, barely sufficient for some crops and wholly insufficient for others. A soil resulting exclusively from the disintegration or crumbling of limestone rocks will be rich in the calcareous element, but deficient in several of the other essentials. Soils resulting largely from feldspathic masses and granite will hold quite all that supply the elements of nutrition to plants, and such are therefore good. No two fields or farms are alike as respects the nature of the soil; and, therefore, when the question occurs, how can this or that farm be restored to fertility, it is necessary to know the general composition of the soil as preliminary to any intelligent attempt to bring it into good tilth. Much of the confusion and doubt which prevail among farmers springs from this difference which exists in soils. Farmers seek for some specific manure which will insure large returns of all kinds; but no such specific exists, nor ever will. There is certainly no specific for our bodily diseases, and therefore doctors in prescribing are said to feel their way in the dark. The farmer who is searching for specifics is groping in thick darkness. The intelligent doctor, who is acquainted with the constitution and the idiosyncrasies of his patient, has a great advantage over one who knows nothing of such peculiarities. The most proper business of the physician is to study the peculiarities of his patients, and the most proper business of the farmer is to study the physical and chemical peculiarities of his soils. Of course, a knowledge of the chemical and geological sciences is of great advantage to a farmer in successfully conducting his labors; but an intelligent observer can secure a good knowledge of the nature of his soils in ten years, and know but little of any of the exact sciences. Without any knowledge of anatomy, of physiology, the farmer obtains by observation a knowledge of the peculiarities of his animals. He learns how to feed his pigs so as to fatten them most rapidly and profitably, how to supply nutriment to his cows so as to cause a copious supply of milk, and he learns the temper and habits of his horses and oxen, and accordingly controls them to his advantage. Why should he not learn by observation the nature and capabilities of his fields, and be able to a great extent so to feed them as to obtain the highest and best crop results from year to year? Any farmer, from ten or even five years' observation, can ascertain the extent to which his different fields are retentive of moisture. He must learn how well they withstand the drought or the protracted wet of summer, how different crops behave when the rain-fall is small or copious in the growing months. Physically considered, some farms are not adapted to the raising of corn, and perhaps some other grains. Corn withstands drought better than almost any other cereal, but that fact affords no reason why it can be raised to advantage on loose, dry soils. Weak, puny corn can be raised in a sand-bank; but foolish indeed would a farmer be to plant his corn in such a locality. Corn requires a good, retentive soil, a good, fine loam, in which to grow in perfection, and if the owner of lands has none such, let him not attempt to grow it. His fields are better adapted to melons, beans, rye, or perhaps wheat. It is useless to attempt to force corn or any of the noble grains to grow upon naturally wet or low clay bottom lands, without thorough drainage and deep tillage. Such are better adapted to grass, and grass farms, if kept in good tilth, are the most profitable of all. Every cultivator of the soil must first become acquainted with the physical character of each parcel he has under his charge, and then he will know what crops are adapted to the several localities.

By drainage and deep tillage, the physical condition of most lands can be completely changed, and with the supplying of such chemical agents as are needed, crops of every description can be raised, satisfactory and remunerative to the husbandman.

WHAT SHALL WE USE FOR WATER-PIPES?

WE are certain that the discussion of no subject can be of more general interest than that relating to the nature and safety of the different kinds of pipes which are used for conducting water to the culinary departments of dwellings. Great anxiety has always been manifested, by housekeepers and others, regarding the safety of the conduit pipes in general use, whether composed of lead or of other metals. It is important that this subject should be fairly and intelligently discussed, in order that the extent of the danger may be clearly understood, and also that the utility and economy of different kinds of pipes may be known. While it is important that all real sources of danger should be pointed out, it is also desirable that groundless or unnecessary fears should be allayed. We are happy to present to our readers, in plain language, the results of several years' observation and experiment upon the different kinds of water-pipes.

LEAD PIPES.

Lead is the metal by far the most largely employed for service water-pipes, and it certainly is the cheapest and most convenient material of which to construct them. It is soft, ductile, easily and readily put in position, and seldom gives trouble by leakage. It is a pity that a metal so well adapted to our wants should be liable to be dissolved by the water brought in contact with it, and that the metal and its salts should so disturb the vital functions as to engender disease and destroy life. And yet, we cannot help remarking, how slight is the danger from the use of lead water-pipes. Millions of pounds of it lie buried in the earth, and through it water is flowing to thousands of families, and yet comparatively a small number suffer from its influence. A large proportion of the waters of this country, that are suited to culinary purposes, will pass through lead pipes under *ordinary conditions*, and remain uncontaminated. During the past quarter of a century, we have studied diligently this matter of the action of different waters upon lead, we have made hundreds of analyses, and have found but few from ponds, lakes, and open reservoirs that do not contain elements which exert a *protective* influence upon the surface of the metal. The first chemical action of water upon lead is usually that of oxidation. The oxygen, which enters into combination with the metal, comes from the air always present in water, or possibly it may come from the water itself through chemical decomposition, the result of galvanic action. The oxide of lead is a soluble compound, and quite poisonous. If the results of the contact of water with lead were to stop here, not a family could use leaden pipes with impunity. The oxide would continue to form as fast as it was washed away and dissolved by the current, and shortly the whole structure would be destroyed. But most waters contain, or hold in solution, another element, carbonic acid, which readily combines with the oxide, and forms a new salt. This is the carbonate of lead, and fortunately is *insoluble*. The first action, then, of most waters upon lead is to form upon the surface a coating of the white oxide of lead; the second action is to change this dangerous soluble oxide into a hard insoluble carbonate, and this, adhering to the whole interior surface of leaden pipes, prevents further contact of the water with the metal, and all decomposition ceases. This is a plain statement of the way in which lead is usually acted upon by water; and if there were no disturbing agencies to come in and interfere with these results, we should hardly require safer or better water-pipes than those constructed of lead.

It sometimes happens that well and spring waters contain other agents which interfere with the chemical changes we have described. Many wells in the Northern States are fed by springs which percolate through or over beds of rocks charged with iron pyrites, or sulphuret of iron. This mineral is usually found in the form of little cubes, very hard and dense, and having a golden yellow color. These cubes are often supposed by well-diggers to be true *gold*. We receive a carefully done-up package of this mineral as often as once a week during the year, sent to us for chemical analysis, the finder believing he has discovered a gold mine. We are always sorry to be compelled to furnish results which demolish the foundation upon which rest "great expectations." Waters brought in contact with such minerals are often impregnated with an offensive gas (sulphuretted hydrogen, or sulphydric acid) and the taste is unpleasant. Their action upon leaden pipes is of an unfavorable nature, producing sometimes rapid decomposition. We have not sufficiently investigated the nature of this action to be able accurately to define it; but it is certain it occurs, and leaden pipes should not be employed to conduct such waters. Organic matter from vaults and cesspools frequently finds its way into wells, and changes the character of waters, so that they become dangerous in their influence upon lead. Some waters are decidedly alkaline, and thus the action of carbonic acid upon lead oxide is neutralized, and it remains in solution.

The nature of the action of water upon lead is changed from local causes, operating within the

WHAT TO USE FOR WATER-PIPES. 139

pipes themselves. Lime, leaves, and other substances, which may be deposited in the angles or bends of pipes, will modify the chemical changes, so as to render an otherwise safe pipe very unsafe. The twisting and bending of pipes, when placed in position, disturb the crystalline structure of the metal, and give rise to electrical currents, which promote its solution in water. Well-waters and spring-waters are usually more unsuited to lead conduction than those of ponds and rivers.

As service-pipes for aqueducts, lead pipes will, under ordinary conditions, deliver water free from lead contamination. In a city or town supply, where the general influence of the waters is protective, as described above, there will be *local causes* operating, through the agency of which *some* families will suffer from lead poison. No city or large town can introduce lead service-pipes into its aqueduct system, with entire exemption from danger. It is not enough to learn the *general* influence of aqueduct waters, as thereby people are misled; we must know the character of the water which flows into each *separate* dwelling, if we would have knowledge of its *exact* influence. If each water-taker in a city could have the water received carefully tested twice during the first year after it is introduced, he would learn whether he is free from danger or not. If, after this period, the water flows pure, no anxiety need be felt. It is perhaps impracticable to have chemical analysis of waters made upon so extensive a scale, but it is the only way in which there can be perfect exemption from cases of lead poisoning in cities. In a majority of wells, lead conducting pipes can be used with safety; but since without analysis it is impossible for housekeepers to know **when** the conditions are unfavorable, it will be better to employ some other kind of pipe. It may be said here that we have used water in our own dwelling for twenty years which passes through leaden service-pipes from the iron mains of the city of Haverhill aqueduct. Not a trace of lead has been found in the water since the first month after its introduction. If we did not *know* that we are free from agencies causing local decomposition, we should remove the pipes at once.

TIN-LINED LEAD PIPES.

To obviate the danger incident to lead pipes, an inventor in New York conceived the idea of lining the interior of such with tin. These pipes are called "*tin-lined lead pipes.*" They are constructed of a thick outside pipe of lead, while another thin one, of tin, is drawn through the interior and rests in contact with it, forming a lining. This idea is such as would quite naturally suggest itself to any one; and ingenious mechanics or inventors, unacquainted with the electro-chemical relationship of metals, would seize hold of it as a most important discovery. They would not know that tin by itself is often more readily attacked and dissolved by water than lead, and that, when placed in association with lead, if any water contact is made between the tin and lead, both metals are dissolved with increased rapidity. We have heretofore unreservedly expressed our dissatisfaction with this pipe; and our views are supported by some *practical* scientific men, whose opinions are certainly worth more than those of a whole army of gentlemen who devote their lives simply to performing illustrative chemical experiments before classes in colleges. Besides this, we have had opportunity of examining specimens of the pipe which have been used for different periods of time, and have found results which fully confirmed our opinions. In regard to this pipe we do not assert that in every case, or in a majority of cases where it is used, it is positively dangerous. If the pipe is perfectly covered with tin throughout its entire surface, and if it is placed in contact with the waters of such wells or aqueducts as do not readily act upon tin, it will serve a good purpose for many years. What housekeepers require in a water-pipe is *not* one which *may become dangerous under conditions liable to occur*, but one which *is safe under all possible conditions. The tin-lined lead pipe is not of this character.*

TIN PIPE.

Pure "block-tin," so called, supplies a good metal from which to construct water-pipes. As noticed above, it has the disadvantage of being readily acted upon by some waters; but this is purely an economical matter, as the salts of tin are not specially poisonous, and no harm can result from its solution in water. Block-tin pipes are quite expensive; but this is a small matter to many, and we recommend the use of tin pipes in cases where cost is not regarded. Of course, there are many who cannot afford them, and a cheaper and equally safe water-pipe is needed. Those who seek a cheaper pipe must not be deceived by the clean, attractive appearance of the

GALVANIZED IRON PIPE.

Iron pipes are "galvanized" by immersing the common gas-pipes in hydrochloric acid, and then immediately placing them in a bath of melted zinc. The zinc amalgamates with the surface of the iron, forming a superficial covering of the metal. This is a *very cheap* process, and was originally adopted with the view of preventing gas-pipes from rusting in damp places. Such pipes were never designed to be used for the conveyance of water, even by the manufacturers; and how any one ever ventured to use them for that purpose is a matter not easily understood. Zinc is a coarse, cheap metal, easily oxidized or corroded by weak acids, and when thus acted upon forms salts which are harmful to the economy. Who ever heard of zinc being recommended by a reputable chemist as a suitable metal from which to construct water-pipes? And yet pipes composed entirely of zinc would be less readily acted upon by water than the coating of the metal when deposited upon iron. The thicker this coating, the more dangerous it becomes, as the longer time is consumed in removing it, and the larger the quantity of salts produced. It may be further observed, that if the salts of zinc were not injurious, galvanized iron pipe should not be used for water from economical considerations. It costs more than plain iron pipe, oxidizes more readily so long as a trace of the zinc remains, and therefore has a less money value. Used for dry gas, above ground, iron pipes coated with zinc may have some advantage over the uncoated, but they are, after all, insignificant. We now pass to the consideration of plain

IRON PIPE.

Water, when it is brought in contact with the metal iron, oxidizes or rusts it more or less rapidly; but it is not rendered poisonous thereby. Neither the oxide, nor any of the salts of iron liable to be formed from water contact, are in the least degree hurtful to the animal economy; and therefore iron conduit pipes are perfectly free from danger under all circumstances. Iron pipes are cheap, easily put in position, are free from the trouble of leakage, and are *safe*. What possible objections, then, can be urged against them? The objections relate wholly to matters of convenience and economy. The rust of iron, which sometimes is formed in considerable quantities, is liable, when the water is used for laundry purposes, to stain clothing; and this causes a good deal of scolding on the part of washerwomen and tidy housewives. Also, tea made of water containing iron-rust is changed into a pale ink; and many vegetables boiled in it are considerably discolored. These are some of the inconveniences resulting from the use of iron water-pipes; but the fact that by rapid oxidation they are often speedily filled up or destroyed may be regarded as the most weighty objection. In some localities and under some circumstances, small service-pipes rust slowly, and will continue intact for many years; under other circumstances, they are soon destroyed. Iron pipes have so many desirable points, we often advise their employment for conducting water to dwellings. No iron pipe of less diameter than one inch should ever be used; those which are smaller soon fill up, and are rendered worthless. A good way to obviate the objectionable feature of rust is to coat the interior with hydraulic cement. The Melrose and Malden Aqueduct Co., who have just introduced the waters of Spot Pond into those towns, are using a cement-lined iron service-pipe, and we predict for it entire success. It is cheap and durable, and oxidation is wholly prevented by this device. Large pipes are now successfully constructed of cement, with a thin iron pipe upon which it rests, interiorly and exteriorly. Pipes of this kind which have been several years in use, continue, we believe, to afford the highest satisfaction.

GUTTA-PERCHA PIPE.

In seeking for a satisfactory material for water-pipes, the curious vegetable substance, *gutta-percha*, has been used to some extent. All metallic contamination is at once entirely avoided by the employment of this material, and apparently it has much to recommend it to favor; but, like a thousand other good things, it has objectionable features. Gutta-percha imparts to water in contact with it an unpleasant taste, and also, in some localities, it undergoes a kind of spontaneous decomposition, by which it is rendered worthless. If, however, these objections did not exist, we presume the item of *cost* would come in to drive it in a great degree from the market. At the present time we think but little of this pipe is used in any section of the country for water conduit.

BRASS PIPE.

Compound metals used for water-pipes must be looked upon with disfavor by chemists. And yet some alloys resist oxidation or other chemical change in a most remarkable manner. We know of no subject which more imperatively demands patient and careful investigation than that of *alloys*. It is a curious fact that aluminum and magnesium, when combined with each other and with other metals in certain proportions, will oxidize so rapidly as to fall into a powder almost instantly; while in other proportions the compound resists the action of oxygen to a degree approaching that of the noble metals. A mixture of copper and zinc may possibly be devised, which, when formed into pipe, will convey water safely; but of such we have no knowledge. A brass water-pipe is now being manufactured and introduced, we learn; but such should not be hastily adopted by any one.

CLAY PIPES.

The common glazed clay or "stone-ware" pipe has been used to a considerable extent for conducting water, and where the pressure is slight it may serve a good purpose. There is a difficulty, however, in securing the sections free from minute orifices which render them leaky, and also it is troublesome to form tight joints. When made of extra thickness, and put in position with care, the clay pipe of small calibre may conduct water under a moderate head, for many years, with great satisfaction. That which passes through will of course be as pure as the mountain or meadow stream at its source, and this is a point of the first importance.

A CARBON WATER-PIPE,

so called, was manufactured and introduced some years since, but we have learned but little regarding its success. It was made, we think, of asphalt and sand principally, and had the merit, at least, of indestructibility. The difficulty and cost of construction may perhaps have proved obstacles in the way of its production; and so it has disappeared from the market. In addition to the varieties of water-pipe described, we may name the glass and the porcelain-lined iron pipes as worthy of notice. Iron pipe has been successfully lined with glass, and we believe the cost was not so great as to prove a bar to its general employment. Nothing could be constructed sweeter and cleaner than pipe of this nature; and we regret to learn that its manufacture has been abandoned in this city. We venture to hope that some one will resume its fabrication, and we feel assured that it might become a profitable business.

We have thus briefly and plainly brought under notice the various kinds of water-pipes which have been used; and the objectionable or desirable features of each have been pointed out.

THE CONCLUSION

of the whole matter may be presented in a few words. Leaden pipes may be employed to conduct water from ponds and rivers or open reservoirs, under *ordinary conditions*, with safety. But since disturbing agencies of a local character are liable to occur, of which water-takers can have no knowledge until evil consequences result, it will be better to substitute some kind of pipe which is safe under all possible conditions. Neither tin-lined lead, galvanized iron, or brass pipes meet this want. Iron pipes are entirely unobjectionable on grounds of safety; and the other undesirable features which have been named are not of so serious a nature as to lead to their rejection for common use as service-pipes. By lining the interior with cement or glass, a conduit pipe is produced which leaves a better one hardly to be desired. Block-tin water-pipes are safe and excellent, but costly. Those who do not mind expense can resort to this pipe for water conduction, with assurance that they are fully protected from danger. It is quite probable that not many years will elapse before new devices for conducting water to dwellings, which are safe and cheap, will be afforded us, as this is an important question towards which many competent and ingenious minds are turned at the present time.

THE CLOTHING WE WEAR.

WE seldom pass through the thoroughfares of a great city without thinking how much the woolen, cotton, silk, and linen fabrics which the crowd of men, women, and children carry about with them upon their persons have to do with their health, comfort, and success in life. Clothing is used not only for warmth, but to secure coolness, and to adorn the person. It also serves an important end in keeping the body clean; for with our ideas of cleanliness, if the whole surface were exposed, it would need as frequent washing as do the face and hands, which we leave bare. In our rigorous northern climate, clothing is worn chiefly for the sake of its warmth; and this is indeed the most important point which demands consideration. The human body is a singular machine, and no function of its complex organization is more wonderful than that connected with the production of animal heat. We are warmed by the process of combustion as truly as are our workshops and dwellings; but the furnace within us is a far more perfect apparatus than anything ever constructed through human ingenuity. The regulation of this internal combustion is so beautiful and exact, that the heat of the body in its normal condition never rises above or falls below 98° F. Place a thermometer under the arm so that it will be fully influenced by the animal heat, and it will rise to 98° and remain thus, no matter whether it be summer or winter. Upon our common thermometer this temperature is marked "blood heat," and it remains a fixed point in the scale. We may take up our residence within the arctic circle, or directly under the equator, and there will be no change in the internal temperature of the body. To keep up combustion, and maintain warmth in our dwellings, we use coal or wood as fuel; the body requires more refined combustible materials, such as beef, mutton, poultry, bread, butter, and vegetables, articles which we class as foods, and which are daily placed under the influence of the digestive processes in the stomach. But the stomach is not the furnace where these substances are burned to warm the body. The fireplace or furnace of the body is in the capillary system, or in the minute, invisible vessels which ramify through every part of the organization. The food we consume is not burned directly, but the tissues which are formed from the food are undergoing the process of oxidation or burning every moment of our lives, and from this burning the body is warmed. Every part of us where blood-vessels are to be formed, every part where nervous influence is perceptible, every organ, every tissue, — muscle, and brain, and nerve, and membrane, — waste away like a burning taper, consume to air and ashes, and pass from the system rejected and useless; and if we did not repair the waste by supplying food, the body would " burn up " as truly as if consumed by a blazing pile. Starvation is a burning process; and those who perish from want of food may be said to die from slow combustion. But we must not be enticed away from the topic which it was our purpose to consider.

Clothing is composed of a variety of materials, and these are used with reference to their influence upon the body. Cotton and linen are cooler than wool or silk, and consequently in this climate we prefer the latter in winter and the former in summer. The former are bad conductors of heat, but the animal products, the wool and the silk, are much worse. Clothing serves the same purpose for the body as coverings of wool or hair felting do for steam or hot air pipes, namely, to keep in the heat, or prevent loss by radiation. The worse conductor any substance may be, the warmer it will prove as clothing. Linen jackets and muslin dresses take the place of cloth overcoats and thick shawls in summer, because they are better heat conductors than the heavy woolen garments. In winter we desire to retain as much animal heat as possible, and so we don the very imperfect conducting substances of wool and silk.

The color of clothing is by no means a matter of indifference. White and light-colored clothes reflect the heat, while black and dark-colored ones absorb it. White is the comfortable and fashionable color for clothing in summer. It reflects heat well, and prevents the sun's rays from passing through and heating the body. If white is the best color for summer, it does not follow that black is the best for winter. It must be remembered that black radiates heat with great rapidity. Give a coat of white paint to a black steam radiator, which is capable of rendering a room comfortably warm at all times, and the temperature will fall at once, though the heat-producing agency remain the same as before. A black garment robs the body of a larger amount of heat than white, and consequently the latter color is the best for winter garments. It is the best color for both summer and winter. Although this statement may seem like blowing hot and cold, it is nevertheless true. Let those who are troubled with cold feet, and who wear dark socks, change to white, and see if the difficulty is not in part or wholly removed. Utility in color is confined to the different shades merging from dark into light; but we find in connection with dress all the beautiful tints of the rainbow, and these are used for the ornamentation of the person. The rich and varied colors which are so extensively worn are by no means to be condemned; adornment of the person to a reasonable extent is commendable. We all love the beautiful in nature, and what adds so much to the attractiveness of woman as the ribbons and scarfs, stained with magenta, mauve, or solferino, which adorn her person? Deep in the instincts of our nature is laid the admiration of color; and we love beautiful flowers and birds and — beautifully dressed ladies.

The abuses in dress must not pass unnoticed. The tight waist, the low necks to dresses, and the high-heeled shoes are most flagrant abuses, and ought not to be longer tolerated. We shall not quarrel with the little jaunty hats of the ladies; for they are indeed pretty, and no harm results from them, as of all parts of the body the head needs the least clothing. But, to pass to the other extremity, we have to say that the detestable high heels to ladies' boots and shoes, running as they do down almost to a point, are spoiling the gait and ruining the ankle-joints of children and young misses. We are careful to order our shoemakers to remove such heels from shoes before permitting them to be brought into our dwelling. Heels of moderate height and good breadth are of great service in elevating the feet, so as to avoid direct contact with moist earth, and they also give support and afford firmness to the step. Why should Fashion push good devices to absurd extremes? We must aid in dethroning the tyrant when her decrees lead to the physical or moral injury of the race. The common fashion of leaving the neck and the upper part of the chest bare, is fraught with evil consequences. It would be less objectionable in countries uniformly warm; but that our daughters, here in this frigid and changeable climate, should constantly expose to chilling winds a vital part of the body, is one of the evils of fashion which should be discountenanced by every mother, and father, and brother.

No part of the dress of men is really more absurd than the hard "stove-pipe" hat so generally worn; and yet all attempts to subvert it have proved abortive. For thirty years we have worn this kind of head covering, and we like it better than any other; we have tried hard to like the low, soft hats, but we cannot; and this is the experience of thousands. Absurd as the high, hard hat is, it does keep the head more comfortable, it does maintain a more equable temperature, it does *feel* better, than any other form of head covering; and so let us continue to knock them against beams in attics and the branches of trees. If they serve a good purpose in brushing cobwebs from the roofs of old garrets and stables, they also protect us from bad bumps, and keep our heads comfortable,

THE RELATIONS OF WATER TO AGRICULTURE.

THE intimate relation which the science of chemistry sustains to agriculture is shown in the fact that all the products of the farm are strictly chemical compounds, and all the changes necessary for their production are chemical reactions of a complex nature. The farmer is therefore but little less than a chemical manipulator engaged in bringing elements into favorable conditions for combination, thus aiding in the production of complex organic bodies. In the spring we place in the ground the little seeds, and in order that the silent chemical forces may operate unimpeded, we furnish in close proximity with the seed those elements which must participate in the reaction, and become integral parts of the future plant. The substances thus supplied we call fertilizers or plant nutriment, and the perfection of the structure depends upon a liberal supply and intelligent application of these elements of growth. These remarks apply to us who are required to till the thin exhausted soils of New England. They have but little significance to that favored class who labor on more perfect soil, where the plant pabulum is present in lavish abundance. Aside from the labor of the husbandman, which is so essential to the growth of plants, there are other forces and agents which are of still higher importance. These are supplied by nature, and are placed beyond our control. Without *water*, all our various forms of fertilizers would remain dormant in the soil. The wonderful solvent powers of water are indispensable in the process of vital chemical action. In itself it is a marvellous liquid. It is so common, so abundant, and enters so universally into all the movements and concerns of life, that we are not often led to reflect upon its chemical composition or its physical properties. Like many other inestimable blessings, its very cheapness and universality remove it from the field of thought, and its extraordinary life-giving capabilities are unrecognized. We can certainly dwell with profit upon a theme so common as common water. The farmer has much to do with the liquid, and it has much to do with and for him. It is safe to say that half of his strength and energy is spent in its transportation from one point to another. The amount of force in the aggregate required to move it during each year, is greater than is expended in all other work upon the farm. In the spring the labor begins by turning up with the plough the heavy, water-impregnated furrows, and in carting from the barn-yard and stable the reeking loads of animal excrement. In these kinds of labor the water is so deceptively combined with earth and manurial substances that its presence is hardly taken into account. It is, however, largely in excess of all other materials, and if we subtract from the cost of force expended through the employment of human and animal muscle this ponderous body, an insignificant sum remains.

Nothing more readily attracts the attention of farmers, or conveys more palpable ideas of value than *bulk*, in manurial substances, and yet nothing is more deceptive or fallacious. A huge bulk of animal excrement under the eaves-droppings of the barn has indeed a positive value, but it does not consist in the great mass of the material of which it is made up. Squeeze out the water, remove the sand and chaff, and we can place all the fertilizing elements of that heap in the smallest sized dump-cart. The high value of stable or barn-yard manure is not found in the eighty or ninety per cent. of water, silica, etc., which it contains, but in the nitrogenous elements, the potash, soda, and phosphatic salts, which in amount occupy relatively a most insignificant position. And I may say further, that the excrementitious salts found in the manure heap have a higher positive value as plant food than any other substance with which we are acquainted. They exist in a form ready to be again taken up by plants and assimilated into the living organism. They differ from the same class of agents found isolated in the hands of the chemist, inasmuch as they have acquired in their passage through vegetable and animal structure, a kind of vitalizing capability, the nature of which is imperfectly understood by chemists.

But the deceptive nature of bulk in fertilizing agents is not confined to barn-yard manure. Leaves, peat, muck, chaff, etc., need to be carefully examined in order to understand their actual value to the farmer. I have made somewhat extended analysis of these substances in order to test the correctness of some published statements regarding them, and also to learn of how much positive service they may be to the farmer. A bushel of well pressed dry leaves, as they fall from the trees in autumn, weighs about four pounds; by further drying, they part with a little more than 30 per cent. of water held in the cells of the leaf structure. A cord of absolutely dry leaves will weigh about 325 lbs., reckoning one hundred bushels to the cord. In weight, then, a cord represents about one twelfth of a cord of wet barn-yard manure, and if they contain the same amount of fertilizing material in the same condition, would be equal in value to that amount of manure. But this is far from being the fact. The dried leaves I have found to stand relatively to the leached organic matter of manure, as 10 to 30, in ash value; and when the soluble salts of manure are taken into account, the comparative value is as 10 to 60, weight for weight. A cord of dry forest leaves, made up of the usual deciduous varieties, maple, beech, oak, etc., has an actual *manurial* value of not over *fifty cents*, reckoning good stable manure at eight dollars the cord. Will it pay to collect them? Certainly not, for the amount of fertilizing material they contain. As litter or absorbents in the stable, leaves have some value, but much less than straw, inasmuch as they lack the reedy character of straw, and because they are far more slowly decomposed.

A pound of good, thoroughly formed peat, taken fresh from the meadow upon my farm, lost a little more than fourteen ounces of water in drying. A farmer drawing from his meadow a cord of peat weighing 4,000 lbs. has upon his wagon 3,500 lbs. of water, and but 500 lbs. of the dry material he seeks. This, dried and compressed, could be placed in a couple of our largest farm baskets. The amount of ash constituents in the pound of peat, after drying, was a little less than 10 per cent.; so that when we reduce the heavy load of peat, which to the eye appears so bulky and valuable, down to its contained inorganic principles, we find the whole amount to be less than 50 lbs. I hope not to be misunderstood in the matter. The ashes are far from being the only manurial part of peat; and as, in burning, some of the most valuable elements are volatilized and lost, it is not good economy to burn peat for the purpose of securing the ashes. Fresh peat, allowed to ferment in contact with lime, is changed into new substances capable of nourishing plants, and where it can easily be obtained it pays the farmer well to secure a good supply. I cannot help remarking, however, in this connection, that many of the statements made by our chemist and journal writers regarding the value of muck or peat are simply absurd, and are proved erroneous by practical experiment. The great value of peat, after all, lies in its absorbent qualities. From the experiments and experience of a considerable number of years, I feel inclined to urge the farmers of our country to save the *liquid excrement* of their animals by the use of seasoned peat in their cattle stalls and manure pits, as an absorbent, rather than to recommend them to drag it many miles at much expense to be used, by itself or in compost, for fertilizing purposes.

In this connection it is proper to say, that one of the forms of frauds practised by manufacturers of commercial fertilizers, is in allowing a large percentage of water to remain in the material, thus adding to its weight. I had the curiosity to examine a specimen of what was called "superphosphate," sent to me last spring by a manufacturer, and it was found to contain 16 per cent. of water. Sixteen pounds in each one hundred would give in the ton 320 lbs., so that a farmer in purchasing a ton of this article receives but 1,680 lbs. If he pays $60 the ton, the water costs him $9.60. This sum goes into the pocket of the manufacturer, along with the very respectable profits resulting from the low cost of most of the materials which enter into the compost. How many farmers, in their purchases of fertilizers, have ever taken into account the item of water which is held in association? In all such purchases they should have in view two considerations: 1st, the quality or genuineness of the material itself; 2d, its dryness or freedom from moisture.

I have said that the labor in moving water upon the farm begins in the early spring. It does not end with that season. There is no body or substance which requires transportation, save rocks and the iron implements of agriculture, into which water does not enter as an important element, gravity alone being considered. The seed dropped in the earth holds it; the earth moved by the hoe or cultivator clings to its associated particles more tenaciously, and requires a greater expenditure of force for its removal. How many tons of water are raised upon the forks, by farmers during the haying season? Grass properly cured has lost half its weight from evaporation, and in the driest hay there remains quite fifteen per cent. of water. Therefore, we stow it upon our mows, and handle it during the cold dry months of winter. The roots and tubers stored in our cellars during the autumn months are but little better than pure water stiffened with a small quantity of starch, albumen, and sugar. If all the fruits and vegetables, so magnificent in quality, and abundant in quantity, which are collected and arranged for an Agricultural Exhibition, were thrown together and placed under a huge hydraulic press, the water held in the juices would float a small yacht, while the pomace could be placed in a large sized market basket. With an ordinary cider press we extract but about half of the liquid which the apple contains.

Among all the products of the farm there is nothing so interesting or wonderful as *milk*. Notwithstanding all that has been written regarding its chemical and physical properties, it is but imperfectly understood by those most directly interested in its production. That there is a want of knowledge of its properties even among intelligent men is shown in the fact that a party of impudent adventurers can establish themselves in our cities, and by advertising find plenty of customers ready to purchase a so-called invention, whereby a pound of good butter is to be made from a pint of milk. If this were accomplished, it would of course be a miracle, equally wonderful with that of our Saviour who turned water into wine. It is certainly as much a supernatural act to change water into butter as to change that liquid into wine. Farmers, clergymen, lawyers, have been made the victims of this audacious fraud. A pint of good milk weighs about 16 oz. If this were placed in a retort and gently distilled, we should obtain about $14\frac{1}{2}$ oz. of pure water; the solid matter remaining in the retort, weighing $1\frac{1}{2}$ oz., holds all the constituents in a pint of milk from which butter can be formed. Milk upon a fair average contains 88 per cent. of water, and consequently the farmer who carries to market 100 gallons of honest milk has in his wagon 88 gallons of honest water, which he honestly sells to his customers, at fair rates per gallon. It seems hardly necessary to carry the attenuation further, by resorting to the pump for more water. There is a popular impression that the water naturally existing in milk, vegetables, fruits, and grasses, differs in some way from that drawn from our wells and springs, but it is essentially the same. The water obtained from the sources named is pure water; that drawn from springs and wells usually containing a few grains in the gallon of organic and inorganic matter, derived from the soil through which it percolates. This is all the difference. From whence comes the water found in milk? Manifestly it is derived from the grasses of the pasture, the hay from the mow, and from the water drank by the animal. This all passes into the economy, and serves to dilute the various active principles upon which its value as food depends. Without dwelling upon those interesting points which relate to the chemistry of milk, let us consider the various forms of food best calculated to promote a copious secretion of the fluid in the animal.

During a period of two years I made some careful and interesting experiments upon a herd of ten cows, which are kept upon my farm. The results of these experiments go to show what a vast difference exists in the value of the feed of pastures apparently similar in soil and situation; also the difference in the green or succulent plants which are grown as food for cows, to be used in the late summer and early autumn months. By changing my herd of animals in the month of June, from one hill pasture to another, only a half mile apart, where the grasses were equally abundant, I found that the falling off of milk amounted in four days to fifteen quarts per day in the aggregate. Upon changing them to the first field, the flow gradually increased, until in about four days it was back again to its original quantity. The experiment of changing the animals was repeated three or four times with corresponding results. The explanation is afforded in the difference which existed in the grasses, in the amount of sweet nutriment which the water held in solution in the circulatory vessels of the plants. The quantity of food was abundant in both fields, and also the clover and the June grasses were produced in both, but in the one the juices were thin and watery, in the other they were richly laden with saccharine and nitrogenous products. The field giving the best results had been under the plough five years previous; the sod of the other had not been broken for twenty years. We do not give sufficient attention to our pastures in New England, and by withholding fertilizing agents, and allowing the sod to become compact and cold, the growths are sadly deficient in the milk and flesh forming constituents. I believe that it pays well to cultivate and give attention to pastures in all our thickly settled districts. One acre maintained in good tilth, so that nutritious and healthy grasses are produced, is worth to the farmer more than three which are suffering from neglect and exhaustion. This matter of securing or providing rich, healthy, green food for milch cows is certainly one of much importance, and should be fully understood by dairy farmers everywhere. We should learn that all edible plants which are green and juicy, and which animals consume with apparent relish, are not necessarily nutritious or profitable as food. We should learn that the richest varieties of grasses and stalks of the cereal grains are dwarfed and even become diseased under imperfect cultivation. The product of a field of clover or timothy grown in deficient sunlight, or under circumstances where there is an excess of soil moisture, or where the plants are crowded, has really a very low money value compared with that of another produced under different conditions of light, moisture, and space. It is a common practice in Eastern Massachusetts, and perhaps in other sections, to grow the corn plant in drills, or in a mass from broadcast sowing, to feed to milch cows late in summer when the pasture grasses fail: a kind of food for animals not profitable to raise; not because the maize plant is not rich and succulent, but because the conditions under which it is grown are unfavorable to its perfect and healthy development. The natural juices of the plant are richly saccharine at maturity, when grown in hills in open space, with plenty of air and light; but grown in mass, in close contiguity, this principle is almost wholly wanting. To test its comparative value with the green stalks taken from the cornfield, I fed to my herd of cows in August a weighed quantity of the "corn fodder," so called, night and morning, for one week; they were then changed to the field corn stalks, and the gain in the milk product at the end of the week was a little over eight per cent., and there was also a manifest improvement in quality. As a rule, all vegetable productions grown under conditions where the chlorophyl, the green coloring principle of plants, cannot be produced in all its richness of tint, are abnormal, immature, worthless. The absence of this principle in the whole of the lower portion of the corn plant grown in drills, or from broadcast sowing, indicates its watery, half-developed character. As fodder for milch cows in summer, the sweet millet, green oats, and clover are much to be preferred to corn, and one or more of them should take its place upon all dairy farms.

The water supplied to milch cows has an important bearing upon the lacteal secretion. With a knowledge of the large percentage normally present in milk, it is natural to conclude that a full supply should be always accessible both in pastures and in yards, and that the quality should be unexceptionable. Muddy, stagnant pools in pastures do not furnish the liquid in proper condition, and as milch cows are generally very fastidious regarding the sweetness and purity of water, they will remain for hours parched with thirst before drinking at such sources of supply. This protracted thirst is fatal to the formation of milk, inasmuch as the animal is rendered nervous and fretful, and water is actually needed to enter into the secretion.

It is a curious fact that cows are often too lazy to go far from feeding grounds to drink, even when the water is pure and fresh. My pasture borders for a half mile upon the beautiful Kenoza Lake, a body of water of unsurpassed purity and excellence, but notwithstanding this, my herd will frequently come to the yard at night in midsummer, actually suffering from thirst. To reach the lake it is necessary to go a few rods through a wooded portion of the pasture, and rather than travel that distance, they are willing to suffer the inconvenience of thirst. The annoyance is so serious that I have determined to open a spring directly in the path leading to the yard.

The location of farmers' wells upon their premises is an important point. How often do we see them located within or upon the margin of the barn-yard, near huge manure heaps, reeking with ammoniacal and other gases, the prolific source of soluble salts which find access to the water, and render it unfit as a beverage for man or beast. It is well known that in the gradual decomposition of animal and vegetable substances at or near the surface of the earth, under certain conditions, nitrogenous compounds are formed. The nitre earths found under old buildings result from these changes. It is, however, quite difficult to understand the precise nature of the chemical transformations which produce them. In the waters of a large number of wells in towns and cities, and also in the country, the nitrates are found in considerable quantities. The salts form at the surface in warm weather, and being quite soluble are carried with the percolating rain water into the wells. Hence it will be understood how important it is to locate wells away from all contaminating influences.

It has long been a matter of surprise to me that instances of impure water are so often found in the rural districts, among those who are not confined to the narrow limits of city lots. In an experience of many years as consulting chemist, I have had a larger percentage of examinations to make of water brought from country homes, than from any other source. The result of these examinations has proved that great carelessness is manifested in allowing sink drains, cess-pools, and excrementitious deposits to exist in close proximity to the water supply, and serious illnesses have been caused thereby. The farmer should make it a point to look carefully after his wells and springs, and permit no possible source of contamination to exist within a broad circle around the spot where they are located.

Water and sunlight are the great agencies upon which the farmer depends for the success of his crops. What a vast amount of anxiety and despondency is caused by these agencies, and yet, they are among the greatest blessings vouchsafed to the race. The excessive heats of summer will parch our fields, and wring out from every tree and shrub the last drop of moisture; and the persistent penetrating rains will drown our cereals, and soak our fields until they are saturated like a sponge. We can do something to mitigate the evils of excessive heat or drought, but we can do much to avert those caused by water. We can drain our soil, and thus carry away in hidden channels the excess of water which, if allowed to remain, would chill or suffocate every root, fibre, and tendril upon which plant life depends.

It is hardly possible to dwell too earnestly upon a subject of so much importance to farmers as *under-draining*. In this country we are not sufficiently awake to the great benefits which flow from it; our faith is not strong enough to lead to the adoption of a system of land-drainage which would overcome one half the losses occasioned by late springs and wet seasons, and which would bring into high tilth thousands of acres now lying waste and valueless. I have upon my farm tested the value of under-drains, not only upon low lands, but upon high lands. Two years ago I resolved to experiment upon a hill or elevation thirty feet above my meadow, and I placed in position tiles, so as to afford a full and free outlet for the water which is so lavishly poured upon us in the spring months. Some of my farmer friends predicted the worst possible consequences to the crop upon that field, and confidently looked for wilted leaves upon the corn stalks during the dry months of July and August. But in this expectation they were disappointed. No wilting came, although the heat was fervid and the clouds gave no rain. The corn planted the first year withstood the drought better than the crops situated upon lower land, and very much better than those upon other fields of equal elevation. It was earlier in starting, grew more vigorously, the product was heavier, and it was harvested much sooner in the autumn than other crops. The second year the same results were observed in the growth and maturation of wheat, and I have no doubt that the improvement is a permanent one — that in a series of years the cash value of the improved crops will greatly outweigh the expense incurred in draining. It is certain that even our uplands can be greatly improved by drainage. What is the philosophy of such apparently paradoxical experiments? It is easily understood. The first great benefit of course comes from conveying away superfluous water at the season when the seeds are placed in the soil. All soils, high or low, are then filled with water struggling to escape by percolation and evaporation, and the farmer must wait until it slowly disappears before putting in his seed. In this there is not only a loss of time, but often it carries crops so late into autumn that early frosts nip and destroy them. This form of benefit is readily comprehended, but the inquiry comes up, "If drains carry away the *unnecessary* water in the *spring*, why will they not carry off the *necessary* water of *summer?* Why do they not leach the soil at the very time when every atom of moisture is needed to feed the growing grains and grasses?" It may be said in reply, that drains are incapable of removing water which is of service to plants; it is only when it is in *excess* and detrimental, that the work of removal goes on. They are active only in wet summers upon elevated lands; their useful services only then come into play. In dry summers they keep the dry soil moist. There is in such seasons reversed action going on. Instead of water coming out, air is passing in, and as even the hottest air holds a vast amount of water, it only needs to be brought in contact with refrigerating substances to produce a copious precipitation of water. All of us have observed large drops of water form upon and trickle down the sides of our ice-pitchers in the hottest days of summer. This water is condensed from the warm and apparently dry air, which comes in contact with the ice-cold surface of the vessel. This will illustrate the way in which the soil is moistened through the agency of drain pipes. The earth, at a distance of one foot from the surface, is several degrees cooler than the air above, and consequently when it passes in through the open ducts, it parts with its hidden moisture, and the vapor is diffused through the soil. Water readily travels through burnt clay, when unglazed. This we know from the fact that if we build a water cistern of bricks, and omit to cover the inside with hydraulic cement, the water will run out as fast as it runs in. The best possible water filter that can be devised is constructed by building inside of a rain water cistern, lined with cement, a brick chamber, which will rapidly fill with water by passing through the bricks. In its passage it is deprived of all impurities and becomes pure and excellent — suitable for all household purposes. A pump passing into the chamber will bring this pure water to the desired point above, and the supply will prove abundant for all ordinary wants. This form of filtration will continue in action for years. I have spoken of the device for a twofold purpose: first, to call attention to a most excellent and convenient way of filtering cistern water, and second, to illustrate the method of action of the ordinary drain tiles. The water passes through the pores in the tiles, and drops are constantly falling from the top arch and passing up from the bottom, through the whole length of the tubes, while resting in wet soils. The minute orifices do not become obstructed as we naturally suppose they would. I have known a brick filtering chamber to supply pure water copiously for a period of fifteen years, and doubtless they will continue in satisfactory action for fifty years.

There is a property in water which is of the highest importance, as upon it all success in agriculture depends. I allude to its solvent power, or its capacity of taking up and holding in solution every substance which enters into the constitution of plants. This singular property is, as it were, the pivot upon which the existence and welfare of the race are poised. Take away from water this power, and no greater disaster could result if the dynamical forces of the universe were thrown into disorder, and the centripetal and centrifugal motions should cease altogether. The rain which falls upon the earth is due to the condensation of aqueous vapor previously existing in the atmosphere, and which is supplied in great measure from the surface of the sea, the area of the latter compared with that of the land being very great, necessarily so perhaps to furnish the requisite extent of evaporating surface. This water is, as is well known, perfectly fresh and pure, the saline constituents of the ocean having no sensible degree of volatility at the temperature at which the vapor has been raised. No sooner, however, does it reach the earth than its solvent powers are brought into requisition, and it becomes contaminated with or takes up a large number of substances, which it holds in solution. The waters of rivers and springs invariably contain a greater or less amount of alkaline and earthy salts, which have been washed out of the earth by percolating rains. In the water we daily use for household purposes, and that which we furnish to our animals, are found considerable quantities of these salts, together with numerous other substances. We are accustomed to regard these as *impurities*, and they are such, strictly considered; but these very impurities are of vital consequence to the living system. These matters exercise an important influence upon the body in health and disease, and if they were entirely absent, physical weakness, and probably death, would ensue. It has been proved by careful experiments upon men and animals, that pure distilled water, so vapid and disagreeable to the taste, cannot be allowed to take the place of impure spring water, without producing emaciation and actual disease. These are very curious and suggestive facts. There is a wonderful provision in nature by which the solvent powers of water are prevented from being injurious to the race. It will be understood that water is capable of dissolving many compounds of the elementary bodies, which are poisonous or prejudicial in their influence, as well as those which are harmless or beneficial. Among the metals, almost the only one the oxide of which is harmless to the living body, is the metal iron. This is held in almost all natural waters. If the oxides of copper or lead were as constantly present in our springs, lakes, and rivers, as iron, our earth would be uninhabitable. The daily absorption into the system of minute quantities of metallic poisons is known to be followed by consequences of a fearful kind. Why are not these poisonous salts present in our natural waters? It is not owing to their insolubility, but to the fact that they are very sparingly diffused through the earth; they are not present in most soils. Iron is everywhere; copper, lead, arsenic, nickel, etc., are confined to specific localities, and are away from the great centres of population.

Lime is a very abundant product in nature, and the water in some sections is charged with it, generally in the form of a carbonate. If another carbonate — the carbonate of baryta — were as common, animated life would fall before its deadly influence. Thus we see the hand of a kind Providence manifested in all the provisions of nature. The consideration of poisonous substances held in water suggests the importance of not doing violence to ourselves, by bringing the deleterious metals, which nature has so wisely placed in remote localities, in contact with water designed for culinary employment. This we are very liable to do, in the use of leaden service pipes. More of the obscure and painful diseases which come under the notice of physicians are due to lead-impregnated water than is generally supposed. Many of these instances are found in the families of farmers, for unfortunately the innovations of fashion and modern improvements have led to the banishment of the old well-sweep and curb, and the copper pump and leaden service pipe have taken their place. It should be understood by farmers and stock raisers that it is not the members of the household alone that suffer from lead-impregnated water; the animals, the cows, the oxen, and the horses, are just as susceptible to its deadly influence as human beings. I have frequently found in my observation in the country, that the stock upon farms was furnished with water conveyed through lead pipes from lakes and mountain springs, while the family with commendable caution drew their supplies from other and safer sources. Many a fine animal has been lost to its owner through the agency of lead poison, and I trust the hint given will not pass unheeded. Iron pipes for the conveyance of water are cheap and safe under all possible conditions, and if those of the capacity of one or two inches are used, they will not soon become obstructed with rust. Never employ what is known as "galvanized" iron pipe, as it is exceedingly dangerous during the first two or three months of service. The superficial covering of zinc upon its surface is rapidly decomposed, and the carbonate and oxide are held in solution or suspension in the water. The salts are hurtful and must not be allowed to mingle with the food and drink.

The vast importance of the solvent power of water will be appreciated when it is understood that it is due to this that all plant structures are able to grow. The aqueous fluid which slowly but constantly during the life of the plant creeps up from the roots, passing through every microscopic cell and fibre, carries along in its current the little atoms of inorganic substances which are so essential to its development. The stream floats not only a great variety of common and well known elements and compounds, but also, in the case of many plants, some of the most rare and curious of which science has any knowledge. Potash, lime, nitrogen, phosphorus, and silica are almost universally found in the sap and substance of plants, and these are the elements which the farmer is desirous of placing in the soil, so that the water may dissolve and convey them in ample abundance to vegetable structures. These are the great essentials, so far as the supply is connected with the agency of water, and they are in a measure accessible, but there are other bodies of the highest importance which it is impossible to furnish. We can supply in a large measure the nitrogenous and other elements which are common to the cereal grains, but we cannot in the case of many of the esculent vegetables. It is certainly remarkable that the common garden beet demands from the water of its circulation one of the rarest of all minerals, rubidium. This metal has only recently been made known to us, through the agency of that marvellous optical instrument, the spectroscope. When and how the water finds and takes up this strange metal, is a problem we are wholly unable to solve. By spectroscopic analysis we are able to detect the thirty thousandth part of a grain of the chloride of the metal; yet it is so sparsely disseminated that even this delicate test fails to give any signs of its presence in soils upon which the beet root flourishes. The growth of the root demands it, and water by some subtle instinct hunts it from the soil and supplies it in the needed quantity. Tobacco is one of the most extraordinary plants which spring from the soil. In its ash is found a class of rare and complex bodies which it has abstracted therefrom, and which are not found in any other vegetable structure. Also, it is a great plunderer of the soil, in respect to those substances which are supplied to it through the ordinary fertilizing agents. The amount of mineral constituents which it carries off can be judged of by carefully examining the ash upon the end of a smoker's cigar. Every 100 lbs. of the dried leaves which the soil produces rob it of at least twenty pounds of its most valuable mineral atoms. This vast amount of mineral the plant pumps up, while held in solution by water. To this plant, potash is what pie or cake is to the schoolboy; it evidently loves it, and consumes it in prodigious quantities. Five per cent. of the dried leaves are composed of this alkali. A bushel of ashes, such as the smoker so carelessly and wastefully brushes from the end of his cigar, would, if leached and the lye formed into soap, make enough to answer the purpose of a small family for a year. The new and rare element, lithium, is found in the tobacco plant, and although the spectroscope will detect in any substance a quantity so infinitesimally small as the six millionth part of a grain, yet it is hardly revealed in soils in which the plant flourishes. These facts open up subjects of thought so interesting and instructive that it is hazardous to enter upon their consideration in the limits of a brief essay. I have only drawn a mere outline of some of the important relations of water to agriculture. It is a subject of almost limitless extent, and may be studied with profit by every cultivator of the soil.

Before closing may I be permitted to ask and to answer the question, What is water? I suppose some of my readers are ready to make the Dogberry-like reply, "Water, sir, is water." That certainly reaches the point by a very short cut, but to the thinking, inquiring man it is not quite satisfactory. Let us answer the question from the standpoint of the chemist. Water is *rust*. The red powder that falls from iron which has long been subjected to the action of moisture is rust of iron. It is the oxide of a metal, and so is water. Water is the rust of hydrogenium, a true metal. This wonderful element no human eyes have ever looked upon, and probably never will, as in its free state it exists only in the form of an invisible gas. Quite recently, science has demonstrated experimentally, what has long been suspected, that hydrogen gas is a metal, and capable of assuming a solid form in alloys. Oxygen, by uniting with this gaseous metal, rusts, oxidizes, or burns it, and water is the rust or ashes. This strange metal, hydrogenium, and its oxide, play an important part in all the operations of nature. It is not alone confined to the little ball of earth upon which we live, but it exists in the stellar worlds above us, and in those misty points of light, the nebulæ, which have so long puzzled and perplexed the astronomer and men versed in the physical sciences. The recent discoveries by means of the spectroscope have proved that this element enters largely into the unformed, chaotic masses of matter, moving in space, of which the worlds are made. It is ready, when the formative act is fully accomplished, of taking its place in combination with oxygen, as water, to aid in the sustentation of animal and vegetable life upon spheres so far distant that our imagination even cannot reach them.

The distant worlds cannot pass from the hand of the Supreme Architect, and be permitted to act under fixed laws, corresponding with those of our planet, until the combustion of the hydrogen which envelops them has taken place, from which are formed oceans and lakes and rivers. We have reason to believe, indeed we have demonstrations and facts to prove, that this is constantly taking place, and that by the agency of fire new worlds are being constantly fitted up on the outermost bounds of space, and made ready probably for the residence of beings like ourselves. Among the stars which have been observed to be on fire, one in the constellation of the Northern Crown, a few years ago, attracted much attention. This very small star, in May 1866, suddenly blazed out and attained a magnitude almost equal to the largest stars seen in the heavens. The spectroscope proved that the light emitted was that which proceeds from burning hydrogen, and consequently water must be the product. This sublime, this awful conflagration, which involved a world much larger than our own, was completed in twelve days, and at the end of that time the star had dwindled and faded away from the second down to the eighth magnitude. I venture to introduce these observations regarding the probable origin of water, because of the intense interest which now invests the subject, and also to call attention to one of the most important and wonderful instruments for scientific research which human ingenuity has ever devised. I allude to the spectroscope. However humble our occupation, or however incompatible with study and research may be our pursuits, we cannot fail to reap the great practical benefits which must flow to us from the labors of thinkers and experimenters, who in the quiet of the study, or amid the dim gases of the laboratory, are extorting from nature her wonderful secrets. As agriculturists, as tillers of the soil, we cannot withhold respect from our scientific investigators; and it will certainly be our fault if our minds and hearts are not improved, and our material interests advanced by the result of their labors. We ourselves must learn to secure a deeper insight into the mysteries connected with our calling, and from the sunshine that is poured upon our fields, the gentle dews that distil upon our grasses, and the drops of rain that gladden and fructify every green thing upon the earth, we must evoke those hidden laws and mysteries, a knowledge of which will guide and aid us in all our undertakings.

THE SKIN AND BATHING.

PHYSIOLOGICALLY considered, it would seem almost impossible to overestimate the importance of the functions of the skin. Consider for a moment the complex apparatus by which these functions are carried on, and the enormous amount of work accomplished through it. If the reader will examine his hand with a simple jeweller's lens, or with any of the cheap pocket microscopes, he will notice that there are delicate grooves crossing the furrows, and that a small orifice exists in the centre of each of them. Some of these orifices occupy nearly the whole of the groove, and are the openings of the perspiratory ducts, from which may be seen to issue, when the hand is warm, minute shining dots of perspiratory matter.

But perspiration is not held in the body as water is held in a sponge, which can be squeezed out by pressure or by throwing it about; neither does it exist ready formed within us, as are the juices in apples and oranges. Upon the under surface of the true skin there are a multitude of little cavities, and in them are minute *glands*, which resemble ravelled tubes, formed of basement membrane and

THE SKIN AND BATHING. 187

epithelial scales, with true secreting surfaces. It is the work of these little organs to receive the impure blood which is constantly brought to them through a network of arteries, and *purify* it; and to thrust out of the system the waste or offensive matter which is separated from it. These impurities come along in the blood, and are cast out through the perspiratory ducts while dissolved in that medium. After the blood is thus cleansed, another set of vessels are ready at hand to carry it back into the interior of the body, to become again and again loaded with impurities, which the little glands are tireless in extracting and removing. What organs in the human body subserve higher or more vital purposes than these? Does the liver or the stomach, or do the kidneys or the lungs, stand in more intimate relation with life than these little glands? We think not. Their size varies in different parts of the body. In the palm of the hand they are from 1-1000th to 1-2000th of an inch in diameter, while in the arm-pits they are 1-60th of an inch. The length of the tube which constitutes both gland and duct, is about a quarter of an inch, and the diameter is about 1-1700th of an inch. It is a curious fact that the ducts, while traversing the true skin, are perfectly straight; but as soon as they enter the tough scarf-skin, they become spiral, and resemble a cork-screw, so that the perspiration is propelled around the tube several times before it is ejected. Now, we are talking about *small things;* but so long as we confine our descriptions to a single duct, we utterly fail to realize their minuteness. Let us look at them collectively. On every square inch of the palm of your hand, reader, there are at least 3,500 *of these perspiratory ducts.* Each one of them being one quarter of an inch long, we readily see that every square inch of skin surface on this part of the body has 73 feet of *tubing,* through which moisture and effete matter are constantly passing, night and day. The ducts, however, are shorter elsewhere; and it will be fair to estimate 60 feet as the average length of the ducts for each square inch of the body. This estimate (reckoning 2,500 square inches of surface for a person of ordinary size) gives for these ducts an aggregate length of 28 *miles.*

The amount of liquid matter which passes through these microscopical tubes in twenty-four hours, in an adult person of sound health, is about sixteen fluid ounces, or one pint. One ounce of the sixteen is *solid* matter, made up of organic and inorganic substances which, if allowed to remain in the system for a *brief space* of time, would cause death. The rest is water. Beside the water and solid matter, a large amount of carbonic acid, a gaseous body, passes through the tubes; so we cannot fail to understand that they are *active workers*, and also we cannot fail to see the importance of keeping them in perfect *working* order, removing obstructions by frequent application of water, or by some other means. Suppose we obstruct the functions of the skin perfectly, by *varnishing* a person completely with a compound impervious to moisture. How long will he live? Not over six hours. The experiment was once tried on a child at Florence. Pope Leo the Tenth, on the occasion of his accession to the papal chair, wished to have a living figure to represent the Golden Age, and so he gilded a poor child all over with varnish and gold leaf. The child died in a few hours. If the fur of a rabbit or the skin of a pig be covered with a solution of india-rubber in naphtha, the animal ceases to breathe in a couple of hours. These statements are presented in order that we may obtain some idea of the importance of the functions of the skin. We have, however, only spoken of one of its offices, that of aeration of the blood; to present the matter fully, we should speak of *absorption*, a matter of less moment, though very important. But we must pass this, and consider briefly the subject of *bathing* in some of its sanitary aspects.

If from any cause the orifices of the perspiratory ducts become partially obstructed or closed, the whole system suffers the most serious derangements. Those important secretory organs, the liver and kidneys, become greatly embarrassed with additional burdens thrown upon them, and a general feverishness pervades the body. This is disease, and the cause of it must be removed, either by bathing the entire surface with water, or by exciting the little glands to unusual activity so as to force a passage through the obstructions. If one pint of liquid material, containing one ounce of solid *excreta*, is thrown out upon the surface of the body and into the clothing every day, it is evident that some care is needed to keep the body clean and the ducts in working condition. In civilized society, this need is recognized, and frequent bathing is resorted to by large numbers of both sexes. The question, "How often should the body of persons in health be bathed?" is an important one, and great difference of opinion exists with regard to it. There is no doubt, however, that bathing, like all other good things, may be abused, and the good we seek from it changed into evil. Many people have been injured by too frequent bathing. As a rule, we regard once a week as often enough for all purposes of cleanliness in persons of sedentary habits, and once in two weeks for those who are engaged in more active in-door pursuits. For those who are at work in the open air, like farmers and some mechanics, the health does not seem to suffer if bathing is resorted to only at quite long intervals, or not oftener than once or twice during the year. A frequent change of the inner garments is of the highest consequence to all persons, and also the thorough airing and changing of bed-clothing. Consider, in the light of the facts we have stated, how uncleanly and injurious is the habit of wearing flannels or underclothing for several consecutive weeks without washing, as very many do. Seven pints of impure liquid, in the form of vapor, pass into the clothing every week from the skin, and half a pound of solid matter accompanies it. Much of this becomes entangled in the fabric, and remains there, a source of impurity, until removed by the labors of the laundress.

Regular bathing, so far as the people of this country are concerned, is certainly a habit of quite modern adoption. The fathers and mothers, and grandfathers and grandmothers, of those who have reached middle life, seldom or never bathed, except in the warm months of summer. Their dwellings afforded no conveniences for the act, if they felt the need of performing it. As a general thing, the health was unaffected by this omission. Why was this? Because of their occupations and their methods of living. They were active workers, they wore but a small amount of clothing, they lived much in the open air, and their dwellings were without stove and furnace heat. If any one in these days will exercise in the open air, so that each day he will perspire moderately, and if he will wear thin under-garments, or none at all, and sleep in a cold room, the functions of the skin will suffer little or no impediment if water is withheld for months. Indeed, bathing is not the only way in which its healthful action can be maintained by those living under the conditions at present existing. Dry friction over the whole surface of the body, once a day, or once in two days, is often of more service than the application of water. The reply of the centenarian to the inquiry, to what habit of life he attributed his good health and extreme longevity, that he believed it due to "rubbing himself all over with a *cob* every night," is significant of an important truth.

If invalids and persons of low vitality would use dry friction and Dr. Franklin's "air-bath" every day for a considerable period, we are confident they would often be greatly benefited. Cleanliness is next to godliness, no doubt, and a proper and judicious use of water is to be commended; but human beings are not amphibious. Nature indicates that the functions of the skin should be kept in order mainly by muscular exercise, by exciting natural perspiration by labor; and delicious as is the bath, and healthful, under proper regulations, it is no substitute for that exercise of the body without which all the functions become abnormal.

DIAMONDS AND DIAMOND CUTTING.

UNTIL within a period of one hundred and fifty years, the East Indies furnished all the diamonds found in the markets of the world. In Hindostan and Borneo the precious gems were found in detached crystals, accompanied with grains of gold, amongst metallic sand washed down from the mountains. When the poor miner who wandered into the mountainous districts of Brazil in pursuit of gold accidentally stumbled upon the famous diamond mines of that country, the whole world was filled with excitement, and the number of miners who crowded thither was very great. The quantity of gems of the very first water obtained from these mines was sufficient to keep the gay and luxurious courts of France and Spain in a blaze of light, as the noble ladies of the time adorned their persons with them. The region of country in Brazil in which diamonds are found is extremely limited. The district of Minas Geraes extends only about eighty miles north and south, and eight from east to west. The character of the earth is an agglomerate, formed by the decomposition of granite and mica slate, and is made up of rounded white pebbles and light-colored sand; in this mixture the diamonds are found along with grains of gold, sometimes crystallized. It is curious that the nature of the earth and the deposits corresponds with that of Hindostan and Borneo where diamonds exist. No one knows how a diamond is produced, or where its natural home is. If its original position is a rocky matrix, as is suspected, it is certain no one has ever seen it. The chemist or mineralogist who will furnish a diamond involved in its primitive home, will certainly shed light upon an interesting scientific problem, and render his name famous. The mountains which supply the *débris* that hold the gems are composed of schistose rocks, intermixed with quartz, sandstone, brescia, flinty slate, limestone, etc. The limestone brescia is the only rock in which diamonds are found in the mountains, and this comprises all we know regarding their original position. By what subtle chemical processes the brilliants have been formed, at some time in the course of those stupendous changes to which our planet has been subjected, we have no knowledge. Undoubtedly fire, water, gases, pressure, etc., have all been concerned in the synthetical work. Chemists have not yet been able to manufacture colorless gems, and it is doubtful if the process is ever understood. In an industrial view, the problem has but little practical importance.

DIAMONDS AND DIAMOND CUTTING.

There is no city or town in the United States where the difficult and interesting process of diamond cutting is carried on but in Boston. In company with Mr. Henry D. Morse, the originator of this peculiar manufacture, we visited the factory where the work is done, and the hour spent in inspecting the process was full of interest. Diamond cutting has been for years monopolized by Holland, and in the city of Amsterdam some *two thousand men* are constantly employed in the industry. With the long experience, however, of these workmen, some of the finest stones are very unskilfully cut, and those brought to this country have been placed in the hands of Mr. Morse to be recut and perfected.

The machinery employed in Holland for polishing is ponderous and heavy, the framework holding the wheels being braced and wedged, like the running gear of a country saw-mill. In the establishment in this city a small iron-top table is used, with solid iron supports and double bearings, so that the polishing wheel, being fixed in the centre, revolves horizontally on a level with the surface of the table. By this ingenious device, the work of Mr. Morse, perfect steadiness is secured, and without the clumsy machinery of the Dutch manipulators a greater degree of accuracy is obtained.

To cut a diamond is to form its surfaces so that

light, in passing through, is refracted in a way to produce a maximum of brilliancy. The rough gems are quite dull or lustreless, and it requires consummate skill in cutting and polishing to secure the accuracy of angular proportion in the faces necessary to perfect results. There must be principal planes or faces, and around them a considerable number of smaller ones, all placed at correct angles, so that, by refraction, a blaze of light, every ray in harmony, may be the result. The skill of the operator is shown in his ability to bring out the *whole power* of a stone.

The diamond is the hardest of known substances, and hence the inquiry will naturally arise, "How is it possible to produce mechanical effects upon a substance so refractory?" "Diamond cut diamond" is an old adage, and it has a practical illustration in the factory. The dust of the gem is employed to wear away the surface of those undergoing the process of polishing, and this is obtained by grinding worthless particles in a steel mortar, and also the minute fragments obtained in the progress of the work are saved for the purpose. But these two sources of supply do not afford sufficient material to meet the wants of the industry, and consequently a substance found in association with diamond, and possessing equal hardness, is to a large extent employed. This pebble, which has no value as a light refractor, is pure carbon, like the diamond, but it is not perfectly crystalline. It is semi-amorphous in structure; and if it was not used for its mechanical value, it would be as worthless as a bit of charcoal. It is now worth in the market about six dollars a pennyweight.

When two diamonds are rubbed together they are mutually abraded or worn away, and hence if we have a valuable one which we wish to cut, to develop its brilliancy, we have only to select another which by its shape is worthless, and bring this to bear mechanically upon the other, and the work goes on. The worthless diamond may be called the tool with which the cutter elaborates the valued gem. Each is placed in cement, conically heaped at one end of two sticks of convenient handling size. The cutter is so placed in soft cement that its cutting angle can be employed to the best advantage upon the clear stone, which is similarly adjusted to present the surface to be abraded. After the cement has hardened, the workman grasps the stick, holding the cutting diamond in his right hand and that with the gem in his left, and the stones are brought together over a double metallic box, the inner section of which is provided with a perforated bottom, being half the depth of the outer, into which it closely fits. The particles which become detached from both stones fall into the inner box, the smaller passing through the orifice, to the bottom, being fine enough to perform their functions on the polishing wheel. The coarser grains are afterwards, as we have stated, powdered in a steel mortar. Diamond cutting is slow and tedious work, and requires the utmost care and skill to accomplish the process successfully. In the Boston factory, the labor is done under the eye or immediate supervision of Mr. Morse, who originated the industry, and who devised and constructed the machinery.

The diamond has a grain or cleavage plane, the same as most mineral or crystalline substances, and hence it is possible to split or divide one into two or more parts. Sometimes a large piece is removed at once from a gem by splitting, but it is a process attended with much risk. To accomplish this after the stone is carefully studied and its line of cleavage ascertained, it is placed in hardened cement, in the proper position, and the sharp edge of a steel chisel resembling a razor is carefully adjusted so that the division will be at the points desired, and a smart rap with a hammer is given it. Perhaps no more costly blow may be struck in any mechanical work than this, for in manipulating a large diamond, if it is unskilfully given, a gem of several thousand dollars' value may be spoiled.

After a diamond is cut, the work of polishing commences, and it is in this department that the

American machinery is seen to be superior to the Dutch. This we have already described. The gem is adjusted in soft lead heaped conically in a copper cup, ten times the capacity of those used upon the cement sticks in cutting. The surface of the wheel is charged with diamond dust mixed with oil to the consistency of thin paste. The stone and wheel thus arranged, the latter is made to revolve at the rate of fifteen hundred revolutions a minute, and the stone, placed in a heavy iron clamp, is inverted upon the wheel. Nothing but the diamond touches the wheel, it being pressed down by the weight of the iron clamp. A rather musical tone is produced by the contact, which shows that the wheel is doing its work, and that now a bright surface will be produced upon the "table" exposed to its action. When this is satisfactory, the operator melts the lead, releases the gem, and readjusts it so as to polish another of the faces, and in this way the process goes on until the work is completed. To attain this, however, the tables and faces are many times exposed to the wheel, and it is not until the most careful measurements and experiments are made that the gem is pronounced satisfactory. Mr. Morse has been intrusted with the manipulation of some of the most costly diamonds ever brought to this country, and in no instance have his labors resulted in loss or failure, a circumstance which reflects much credit upon his ingenuity and skill.

The importation of African diamonds has but just commenced, but doubtless large quantities from the new mines will flow towards this country, as we are large purchasers of the "brilliants." The market in the United States will not put up with anything but the best. We do not purchase the largest, but the choicest which are produced in all parts of the world. Stones of from one to five carats are always in good demand here; above that, purchasers are scarce. A seven or ten carat diamond is worth from $6,000 to $10,000, and the number of those who are willing to invest that sum in a single stone is limited. Sporting men, who keep gambling saloons, and drive fast horses, wear the largest and most costly gems; and when we notice an unusually large and brilliant one upon the person of a stranger, we instinctively regard him as belonging to the sporting fraternity.

In what is known as the "shoddy" era, during the war, when petroleum and war contracts elevated men suddenly from poverty to great affluence, large diamonds were in demand, and there were not enough of these in the country to meet it. The price of diamonds of one carat ranges from $165 to $175, but there are some "unexceptionable" ones in the market which command a higher price. Most of those who visit jewellers' stores for the purpose of purchasing diamonds have no knowledge of the nature of the gems they seek. They do not know that a diamond, like a horse or an oil painting, is sold for its excellence or beauty. If a diamond is "off color;" or even has slight flaws, they do not detect the faults. If diamonds are sought, it is important that they should be purchased of honest parties, and those who by experience are fully acquainted with their character and value.

It is certainly singular, that with the immensely increased production the gems continue to increase in price from year to year. The recent convulsions in Europe, and our late civil war, in which thousands of diamond owners were reduced to penury, did not result, as one would suppose, in throwing upon the market large quantities of diamonds. It is probable a few changed hands, but not enough to influence the price in the slightest degree. Large numbers of the diamonds which have been dug from the earth in the last two thousand years have been hoarded, and are not often brought to the light. They are left to dazzle unseen, in caskets and steel safes, where they are almost forgotten. A diamond worth £30,000, or $150,000, has recently been found in the African mines, and several others of a size and brilliancy which render them nearly as valuable are reported. It is highly probable that diamonds in considerable quantities will be found in the United States at no distant day. In the mountains of South Carolina and Georgia, where gold exists, there are geological strata which present striking analogies to those of Brazil, Africa, and Australia where diamonds are found in abundance. A few have already been picked up in those localities, and also in California.

AMONG THE COAL MINERS.

THERE is no more picturesque or interesting region of country in the United States than that in which are found the anthracite coal-beds of Pennsylvania. In many respects it is more attractive than the mountain regions of New Hampshire, or the Adirondacks of New York, and it is equally accessible. Upon entering this section from New York, by way of the New Jersey Central Railroad, the first remarkable point reached is the town of Mauch Chunk, a name which few dare attempt to pronounce without first taking lessons in the feat from some one of the residents of the place. Correctly interpreted, it means "Bear Mountain," an Indian name for a lofty peak ascending from the valley. Mauch Chunk lies in a narrow gorge between and among high hills or mountains. This gorge is quite narrow, and the scenery is wild and grand. The little Lehigh River, arrested in its course by dams, canal locks, and rocks, foams and frets on its way through the defile, and the scream of steam whistles, the rumbling of innumerable trains of cars, and the shouts of boatmen, make up a chorus of noises, day and night, altogether unusual. The town is so wedged in by the hills that only one narrow street is practicable, and the whole space is taken up by the walled river, the canal, railroads, street, and line of houses. No place on earth presents so many interesting and wonderful points connected with the coal interests, as Mauch Chunk. Standing upon the balcony of the hotel, and looking out upon the mountains, they seem to be alive with long trains of coal cars. These are not confined to the valley, but are seen far up the sides of the mountains, and upon their very tops, at an altitude of twelve and fifteen hundred feet. They shoot along, looking like huge serpents, winding around among rocks and trees, and by deep chasms, and over trestle-work supports, carrying their heavy loads of black diamonds to the waiting cars and boats below. The trains not only run along upon horizontal pathways, but up and down the mountains, upon inclines which seem almost perpendicular. At the highest points are huge stationary engines which draw up the long trains of empty cars with the greatest despatch.

The starting-point of what is known as the "Switch Back" railroad, is at Mauch Chunk, and a most unique and wonderful road it is. It was not designed for passenger travel, but solely for the conveyance of coal from the mountain mines, about nine miles from the town. An enterprising gentleman some time ago obtained permission of the owners to run an excursion train over the road twice a day; and parties are now taken over the route in comfortable little cars, without locomotives or driving power of any kind. To reach the road proper, it is necessary to ascend to the top of Mount Pisgah, a precipitous dome in front of the hotel upon the opposite side of the river, and about thirteen hundred feet high. We take an omnibus, which carries us up four hundred feet to a niche in the mountain, and here stepping into the car we are drawn up at an angle of forty-five degrees to the top of Pisgah, nine hundred feet higher. On the very apex of the mountain the stationary engine is placed, with two huge smoking chimneys, which give to the mountain the appearance of a volcano. We started from this elevation on one of the loveliest mornings in June, to make the circuit of the "Switch Back," or what is sometimes more properly called the "Gravity Road," and this carries us over an extent of twenty-five miles upon the tops and sides of mountain ranges. Our first stage is down a gentle decline of nine miles to the foot of Mount Jefferson, up which we are drawn by another stationary engine. The way is now a downward grade until we reach Summit Hill, when we descend rapidly into the valley, where most of the coal mines in working condition are found. This is a sequestered, romantic place, apparently as far out of the world as any one would ever desire to visit. The great coal breakers are upon the right hand and the left; and dark, yawning pits, the entrances to the subterranean passages traversed by the coal diggers, are seen in every direction. Mountains of coal dust, the refuse of the breakers, project into the valley, and give a sombre hue to everything. Even the leaves upon the trees become darkened by the coal dust; and black, turbid streams wind around among the rocks, seeming anxious to escape from the dingy caverns in which they originate. From the "slopes" or entrances to the mines, mule teams attached to trains of cars, loaded with coal, are constantly emerging; and the drivers in charge, with oil lamps affixed to their caps, and begrimed with the sooty powder, seem like mountain imps who have no business with daylight or the outside world.

Before proceeding to speak further of mines and coal mining, let us return to the road by which we came into this region. Shortly after leaving the valley, another mountain opens before us with its smoking chimneys at the apex, and up this we are drawn at a rapid rate. From this high point our return route commences, and we run over the track at a fearful speed until we reach the town of Summit, the home of the miners, which has a church, school-houses, and barracks for troops, as it has been found necessary in turbulent times to quarter a regiment of soldiers at this point to preserve order. The track the whole way is a down grade, and an hour's ride brings us back to the base of Pisgah, our starting-point. During the ride of twenty-five miles we have been seated in our little car by the side of the conductor, whose sole business has been to keep his hands upon an iron wheel which controls the brakes, and governs our rate of speed. We look out of the open door in front, and our view is unobstructed by engine or tender, for we travel independent of both; no smoke, gas, or steam whistle annoys us, and we rush along, propelled by an unseen power, a force which is potent, but inexplicable. It is impossible to realize the true nature of the track, for the descent is very gradual, and it appears like an ordinary level road, high up among the clouds. We presume the excursion is not peculiarly hazardous; but it must be confessed it seems so, at least during the first half dozen miles of travel; we could not learn that any serious accidents had occurred during the time the road has been open to excursionists, and it is probable that every precaution has been and will be used to prevent them. This railroad in many respects is as wonderful as that constructed up the bare side of Mount Washington, and even more interesting. The steep declivities are, however, surmounted by the aid of stationary engines at the tops, whilst tne cars on the Mount Washington road are accompanied by the unique little locomotive, which lifts with its arms of iron behind, and forces the train up the almost perpendicular rock to a height of nearly seven thousand feet. We can never cease to wonder at and admire such triumphs of mechanical and engineering skill.

A hunter named Ginter first discovered anthracite coal in this region, eighty years ago; but he did not understand its nature, and it was called "black stone," and supposed to be as incombustible as granite. The history of the early attempts to burn anthracite are not only amusing but instructive, as they serve to show how mankind may be baffled in attempts to reach an end as easy and simple as building an anthracite coal fire. It required more than *forty years* to learn how to burn this form of fuel; and it is alleged that the discovery was made accidentally after all. An experimenter in Philadelphia, after most persistent efforts to ignite the black stones, gave up in despair, and left his furnace filled with a mixture of wood and coal, and went home to dinner. Fortunately there were some sparks left upon the wood, and more fortunate still, the furnace door was left *closed*, with the draft *open*. This arrangement afforded the necessary "let alone" treatment, and the wood, soon igniting, heated the coal to a point where it also could be ignited; and as the downcast experimenter returned to rake out and throw away the supposed worthless coals, he found them to his surprise all aglow, and causing such intense heat that his furnace was well-nigh destroyed. This result of course dispelled the idea that anthracite was an incombustible substance; and soon companies were formed to work the mines. Coal was, however, brought from this region by slow and wearisome modes of conveyance, such as by wagons, and on mules' backs, until 1827, when an imperfect track was laid to run cars down the mountains by gravity, and in this originated the present very remarkable "Gravity Road."

But let us leave Mauch Chunk, and by the Lehigh and Susquehanna Railroad travel up the wild gorges of the mountains through which the Lehigh River forces its way, and when we have reached the summits, we will descend into the beautiful Valley of Wyoming. This broad, fertile basin, with the rim of mountains bounding it upon every side, is indeed a charming retreat; and no wonder the poor Indians in the early days of our history were reluctant to give it up to the rapacious white men. Here every inch of ground rests upon a support of anthracite, for the valley and surrounding hills are full of it, and it crops out at various points, showing what a wealth of the mineral reposes below. Scattered up and down the valley are seen the huge coal breakers, which dot the landscape almost as thickly as do the windmills in Holland. Coal, coal, nothing else but coal is thought of or talked about, and the pretty city of Wilkesbarre is the centre of the great industry. We are pleased to accept the kind invitation of Mr. J. H. Swoyer to visit the celebrated Enterprise Colliery, in Pleasant Valley, which is under his direction, and witness the operations of mining, crushing, screening, and preparing coal for the market. With Mr. Patten, the gentlemanly superintendent, for a guide, we descend the "slope" and penetrate into the side of the mountain, and grope our way through the grim passages made by the miners in order to reach the deep coal seams, hundreds of feet below the surface. Small cars, black as the coal itself with dust, rumble along the excavations, drawn by mules, conveying the coal to the great shaft over which is built the breaker, and here it is hoisted by steam power up to daylight. The reflection occurs that this remarkable substance, which is in itself only solidified sunlight, has rested in its dark abode for uncounted ages, and not a beam of light has shone upon it until to-day, since the floods of the carboniferous epoch swept it into these basins as vegetable matter, and covered it with the silt and mineral *débris* which were forced along with it in its course. We are led to regard it as a kind of *pemmican* fuel, and here is the vast *cachet* established by the Infinite One, from which we can draw unlimited supplies.

The Enterprise Company are at present working upon a seam a little less than five feet in thickness, which is about the least that can be worked with profit. The coal *in situ*, as we look upon it by the dim light of the miners' lamps, appears as a dark, shiny stratum, tightly compressed between heavy masses of shale and limestone. The weight of the mountain seems to rest upon it, holding it as in a vice. To dislodge or break it from its bed is the work of the experienced miner, and this is accomplished with wonderful tact and skill. A sharp drill is used, by which orifices are made in the seam, and when these are filled with gunpowder, tamped, and exploded, large fragments are dislodged, which are placed in the cars by the laborers, and drawn through the dark labyrinths to the shaft. The regular miner never lifts any coal for carriage; this is the work of the *laborer*, and entirely beneath his dignity. As we entered the mine at about noon, several miners were met coming out, and we were informed by the superintendent that they had completed their day's work, and had the afternoon to themselves. They had dislodged as much coal from the bed as the laborers could load and carry away during the day, and their task was completed. There is an aristocracy in these subterranean abodes as exclusive as any found above ground, and "consuming ambition" finds as full play in the breasts of the little sooty colliery boys, as in those met with in our schools or employed in our counting-rooms. The boys born of the men at the mines care but little about books, and dream of no other occupation than mining. At an early age they go into the breakers, and take their first step in the business in picking out the fragments of slate that fall through the meshes with the coal in the process of screening. From this they look forward with earnest desire to the time when they can go into the mines and drive the donkeys attached to the coal cars; from this they wish to become laborers, and load the coal; and the crowning summit of their ambition is only reached when they become miners, and are fully connected with the "ring," and under full pay.

The mines are filled with the smoke of gunpowder; but after a short stay it is not oppressive. The work of mining, viewed from our stand-point, is not an agreeable occupation, but it is less exacting and laborious than many other kinds of labor. It is also less hazardous than many other pursuits, although a contrary notion prevails. The perils incident to the sea are far greater; and also many industrial pursuits, such as the making of gunpowder, matches, pigments, etc., are more destructive to life than coal mining. There have been in this country only two very serious casualties: that of the Avondale mine, and the more recent one at Pittston. There are employed in the anthracite region about thirty thousand miners, and the loss of life from accidents incident to the business shows but a very small percentage. It is the terrible *nature* of the casualties, when they do occur, that awakens such wide-spread sympathy, and causes the occupation to be looked upon with dread.

The masses of coal raised from the pits are carried far above the opening of the excavation, and thrown into the breaker, a ponderous iron machine, which crushes them to fragments of various sizes; and then they fall into revolving cylindrical sieves, the meshes of which determine the size of the coal manufactured. In this manner, the "egg," "nut," and "bean" coal are separated, each sieve sifting out its appropriate size, and directing it into different receptacles. At some of the mines one thousand tons of coal are raised and broken in a day, and the aggregate of the amount produced is prodigious. The profits of the business, as conducted at the mines, seem reasonable, as we were informed by one of the largest producers that he was entirely satisfied when he could realize twenty-five cents profit on each ton delivered. A vast monopoly has virtual control of our anthracite coal-beds, and what the future may develop it is impossible to foretell. A comparatively few very wealthy men in our large cities are the owners of the mountains and valleys where lie hidden the precious deposits of coal, and upon them depend in a measure the development of our great national industries. At present it is not for the interests of owners to attempt to combine or monopolize, but how long this may continue is a question of no little national importance. The supply *is vast* in amount, practically inexhaustible, — and this fact affords reasonable assurance that centuries may elapse before any measures may be taken to force prices to a point where they will be restrictive, or very oppressive. The high prices of coal which have ruled during the past two or three years are caused by occurrences independent of ownership of the coal lands.

CHEMISTRY OF THE HUMAN BODY.

IF we could subject the body of an adult person, weighing 154 pounds, to the process of chemical analysis, and then set down the results in the usual way, it would read about as follows:—

	lbs.	oz.	grs
Oxygen	111	0	0
Hydrogen	14	0	0
Carbon	21	0	0
Nitrogen	3	8	0
Phosphorus	1	12	190
Calcium	2	0	0
Sulphur	0	2	219
Fluorine	0	2	0
Chlorine	0	2	47
Sodium	0	2	116
Iron	0	0	100
Potassium	0	0	290
Magnesium	0	0	12
Silicon	0	0	2
	154	0	0

The oxygen and hydrogen, for the most part, are combined in the body in the form of water; of this compound there would be about 110 lbs. The carbon is mainly contained in the fat; the phosphorus and calcium exist in the bones; the other minerals, in the juices of the flesh and in the blood. Of course the statements as given are but a rude approximation to the truth, but they are, nevertheless, sufficiently exact to afford a tolerably correct idea of the nature of the substances, and the amounts which enter into the human organization.

From this presentation it will be seen that the body holds sufficient water at all times (about 14 gallons) to drown the individual, if it were contained in a suitable vessel. Under ordinary circumstances six pints of this water leave the system each day. If we drink largely, of course an increased quantity is eliminated through the excretory organs. This liquid finds its way into the system through the food and drink. Considerably more than half the bulk of all the bread, meat, and vegetables used as food is water. There is no other substance but water which remains unchanged after entering the body. Under the terribly destructive influence of vital chemical action, all other agents and bodies are torn asunder, and from their elements are formed new compounds of most strange and complex natures; water flows through our life, as it flows from mountain cataracts and meadow springs, unchanged and unchangeable, save in its physical aspects and condition. It is made capable of holding in solution all the nutrient and effete principles which enter or which are rejected from the human organization, and it is the medium through which it is built up and torn down. Life and death are alike dependent upon its agency.

Of phosphorus, every adult person carries enough ($1\frac{3}{4}$ pounds) about with him in his body, to make at least 4,000 of the ordinary two-cent packages of friction matches, but he does not have quite sulphur enough to complete that quantity of the little incendiary combustibles. This phosphorus exists in the bones and in the brain, and is one of the most important constituents in the body. Every schoolboy is acquainted with those strange metals, sodium and potassium, for he has seen them flash into a brilliant flame when thrown upon water. The body contains $2\frac{1}{4}$ ounces of the former, and a half ounce of the latter metal; enough for all needed experimental purposes in the schools of a large city. The 12 grains of magnesium would be ample in quantity to form the "silver rain" for a dozen rockets, or enough to create a light which under favorable conditions could be seen for a distance of twenty miles.

Our analysis disproves the old vulgar notion, that the blood of ten men contains iron enough to form a ploughshare. The 100 grains of metallic iron found in the blood of a healthy adult would be sufficient to make a good-sized pen-knife blade, but no useful implement of a larger size. There is one important element associated with iron in the blood, which does not appear in the "analysis," and that is manganese. This element has not been recognized until a comparatively recent date, and its importance has been strangely overlooked.

Probably no fact in medical or chemical science is more widely understood than that there is "iron in the blood." As a fact it is no more remarkable than that this fluid holds potassium or sodium, or that the brain is permeated with phosphorus. The popular curiosity and interest regarding iron as it exists in the circulation have been excited by the venders of quack remedies alleged to contain some combination of the element. While there is much that is very absurd in the statements popularly presented, it is impossible to overlook the importance to the well-being of the individual of the few grains of iron found in the blood. If the quantity is diminished from any cause, the whole economy suffers serious derangement. We have reason to believe that when the normal quantity (about 100 grains) is reduced 10 per cent. the system is sensibly affected, and the health suffers. How sensitive to all the chemical reactions going on within and around, is this complex machine which we call the body!

But iron, among the mineral constituents of the body, does not stand alone in its important relationship. The metals exist combined with other bodies, or they are locked up in the form of salts, which are vital to the economy. There are five pounds of phosphate of lime, one of carbonate of lime, three ounces of fluoride of calcium, three and a half ounces of common salt, all of which have important offices to fill. Not one of them must be allowed to fall in quantity below the normal standard. If the lime fails, the bones give way; if salt is withheld, the blood suffers, and digestion is impaired; if phosphorus is sparingly furnished, the mind is weakened, and the tendency is towards idiocy.

Whence do we obtain these extraordinary metals and mineral substances which are diffused through the body? It is certain that among the dishes found upon our tables, none contain phosphorus, lime, iron, or magnesium, in their isolated condition. In the food we daily consume these minerals are found, and they constitute a part of the materials of its structure. A pound of wheat, of which we make our bread, holds a quarter of an ounce of mineral substances; a pound of potatoes contains the eighth of an ounce; cabbages, lettuce, apples, pears, strawberries, etc., also contain considerable quantities. Beef and other meats contain about four pounds of minerals in each hundred, and in the juices there are certain remarkable agents which are crystallizable, which have an alkaline reaction, and which unite with acids to form salts. These are creatine, creatinine, osmazome, etc. We hardly know where to class these agents, but they are undoubtedly of the highest importance in nourishing our bodies.

In case of deficiency of mineral compounds in the economy, it is possible to supply a part of them by the use of the substances themselves, but there are others which can enter only through the food.

Common salt (chloride of sodium) furnishes directly and readily the sodium salts and compounds. Iron can be supplied to the blood by administering it in various forms and combinations, or by giving the pure metal in powder.

Perhaps lime in some of its soluble forms is assimilable, and the same may also be said of phosphorus, as held in the weaker chemical combinations, as in hypophosphorous acid, and in the alkaline hypophosphite salts. If invalids who need the lime and phosphorus compounds would use whole wheat bread, they would secure the mineral food in a perfectly natural way. In the outer covering of the wheat berry, for some good reason, those elements are mainly stored up, and if we sift out and throw away the bran, we deprive ourselves of a most essential portion of the grain.

In the extract of beef, or in the isolated juice of beef, are found enormous quantities of minerals in a perfectly assimilable condition. In one hundred pounds of good dry extract of beef, made by evaporating the juices, there are contained twenty-one pounds of the most important agents needed in the animal economy. We would suggest to physicians and invalids the use of this beef extract in all cases where the system is suffering from deficient nutrition, or where there is any weakening of the vital powers through an insufficient supply of the mineral or nutritive agents essential to perfect health.

ABOUT QUICKSILVER.

IN adapting material things to the uses of man, it was doubtless regarded as necessary that one mineral substance should be constituted so as to remain in a *liquid* state under all ordinary conditions. The metal thus provided for us is quicksilver or mercury. We remark that it is liquid under *ordinary* conditions of temperature, for it should be understood that under extraordinary conditions *all* metals are liquid. It is well known that the atoms of iron, steel, copper, platinum, etc., which are associated in heavy, refractory masses, are not so immobile, or fixed, as they appear to be, for when submitted to high temperatures they run like water. Subject quicksilver to a temperature sufficiently high to render iron *liquid*, and it instantly becomes *vapor*, and will float away like steam. Iron, when subjected to a heat capable of liquefying platinum, will itself become vaporized, and platinum in its turn is vaporized by a higher heat, and so all the metals are physically changed under the influence of heat. There is not a solid substance upon our globe, not a mineral or metal, that has not existed probably for millions of years in the aeriform state, a condition resembling steam or air. If quicksilver is carried within the Arctic Circle, it no longer remains liquid, but becomes solid, and can be hammered, like lead or copper. The ordinary temperatures under which man flourishes upon our planet are alone favorable to the existence of this singular liquid metal. Is not design clearly discernible in this? Is it not clear, in order that certain arts and art processes of benefit to the race should be established and carried on with facility, that a heavy, dense, liquid metal, like quicksilver, was needed? Possibly the world *could* have got along without it. Our non-mercurial barometers and thermometers might have been invented, the photographic process discovered, and impalpable gold dust separated from its parent rock through some other agency. It must be admitted, however, that quicksilver has served an important, if not indispensable end, in originating and perfecting these instruments and processes. There are plenty of pretentious charlatans who are busy declaiming against its usefulness or safety in medicine; but, nevertheless, mercury *is* a most important therapeutical agent. Like all good things, its employment, if directed by ignorance or carelessness, may result in injury rather than benefit; but wisely and judiciously used, it subserves important curative ends, — ends hardly reached by any other known agent. The popular prejudice, engendered by designing quacks, against the use of mercury in medicine, is not founded upon justice or intelligence.

The amount of quicksilver which the various mines of the world are capable of furnishing is very large, — much larger than is demanded for any purposes to which it is at present applied. The quicksilver mines of California alone could furnish fifty times more than is consumed in the whole world, and the same may be said of the old Almaden mines of Spain. The discovery of a new quicksilver mine in the United States, no matter of what extent or richness, would possess but little more value than that of a common clay bed, if it was attempted to be worked in competition with existing mines in California and Spain. The price would immediately run down to a point so low that its extraction must cease. At present the quicksilver trade of the world is substantially an armed truce between Spain and California. By a kind of tacit understanding between the controllers of the products from the two sources of supply, Spain is allowed to furnish the London market and nearly the whole of Europe. Until within a few years it had the great Chinese market also, but California, by adroit management, has driven Spain out of the Celestial Empire, and now claims that as her territory. In the present attitude of the trade, if California should ship 10,000 flasks to London, and offer it at a reduced price, Spain would ship 10,000 to New York, and down would go the price there. On the other hand, if Spain sends a ship-load to New York, California goes to London, and so very shortly the whole business would end in ruin. To maintain remunerative prices, there must be but a limited amount distilled, and there must be special markets for the products of the two rival mines. We have spoken of California as if possessed of but a single mine. This is not to be understood as literally true. California has several mines of considerable importance, but the operations of the one known as the "New Almaden" are much the most extensive. Great as are the resources and wealth of the New Almaden quicksilver mining company, they could not continue business for a single year, if they did not accede to a combination with the weaker New Idria and Redington companies. This combination now controls the production and price of quicksilver, and when they agree that it shall go higher or lower, it fluctuates accordingly. It is, however, for their interest to keep the price uniform, and not unreasonably high, and so there is found but little variation in quotations in the great central markets.

The total annual supply from California is not

far from 50,000 flasks, or about 3,000,000 pounds. This is used in metallurgy, manufacturing, and art processes. The largest quantity is used by the gold miners in the amalgamating process at the various mines. A considerable amount is used by manufacturing chemists in preparing calomel, "blue pill," mercurial ointment, and various mercurial salts and plasters. The Chinese make from quicksilver that beautiful pigment, *vermilion*, which is so largely employed by painters and colorers in all parts of the world. It is singular that this half-civilized people are able to prepare a chemical compound from quicksilver, which is superior to, and which commands a higher price than the same salt produced in Europe and the United States, where the arts are carried to the highest perfection. English and American vermilion, as found in the market, is far inferior in brilliancy and quality to the Chinese.

One of the most curious properties of quicksilver is its capability of dissolving or of forming amalgams with other metals. A sheet of gold foil dropped into quicksilver disappears almost as quickly as a snow-flake when it falls into water. It has the power of separating or of readily dissolving those refractory metals which are not acted upon by our most powerful acids. The gold and silver miners pour it into their machines holding the powdered gold-bearing quartz, and although no human eye can detect a trace of the precious substances, so fine are the particles, yet the liquid metal will hunt it out, and incorporate it into its mass. By subsequent distillation it yields it into the hands of the miners, in a state of virgin purity. Several years ago, while lecturing before a class of ladies upon chemistry, we had occasion to purify some quicksilver, by forcing it through chamois leather. The scrap remained upon the table after the lecture, and an old lady, thinking it would be very nice to wrap her gold spectacles in, accordingly appropriated it to this purpose. The next morning she came to us in great alarm, stating that the gold had mysteriously disappeared, and nothing was left in the parcel but the glasses. Sure enough, the metal remaining in the pores of the leather had amalgamated with the gold, and entirely destroyed the spectacles. It was a mystery, however, which we could never explain to her satisfaction.

EXPERIMENTS WITH AIR FURNACES.

DURING the past winter we devoted considerable time to the investigation of the mechanism and operation of air furnaces, with the view of ascertaining by practical experiment the nature of the defects so generally complained of; and we also entertained the design of attempting to remedy these defects. What are known as "portable furnaces" are now largely used in all houses of moderate dimensions, and as these in no respect differ in construction from the kinds placed in brick chambers in large houses, attention was given to this form of apparatus. After a full examination of the various popular devices offered by manufacturers, two were selected as embracing the most sensible and desirable features in form and construction, and these were subjected to practical trial. It should be observed that all the various patented contrivances found in the market are in many particulars essentially alike. The "improved" kinds, or those quite recently invented, appear to be more objectionable in construction than others which have been longer known. In the newer devices, the inventors seem to think that the merits of their apparatus consist in a multiplicity of tubes, "return drafts," flues, chambers, dampers, etc. They are for the most part as intricate as Mrs. Chauncey's celebrated new cooking stove, which required a whole cord of wood to warm all its mysterious windings and passages; and even after this expenditure of fuel, she declared she could not retain heat enough in the machine to bake her morning biscuit. All furnaces found in the market have the radiating surfaces in the air chamber constructed mainly of *cast-iron*. They all have more or fewer joints, formed by placing together pieces of metal, which are filled with some kind of lute or cement, when the furnace is placed in position. The air is allowed to pass in beneath the base, and around the ash-chamber and fire-pot; and usually the current of air is unobstructed by any devices to retain it in contact with the radiating surfaces.

The two furnaces subjected to trial may be regarded as representative devices, and combining as many good qualities as any offered for sale by dealers. The first was put in position in a basement, and arranged for warming a library, a room forty feet long, twenty wide, and eleven high. It was kept in place for five weeks, and its working diligently attended to. With the aid of proper instruments, thermometers, hygrometers, etc., and chemical reagents, results regarding temperature, moisture, and the presence of gases and extraneous bodies in the room, were carefully noted. The furnace was then removed, and the other one put in its place. The same experimental labors were undertaken with this during a period of four weeks. As the details of these experiments require for their proper presentation more space than can be afforded in this essay, we will only allude to them in general.

The interior of the furnaces was made of cast-iron, and the joints of the first were cemented with a paste made of finely pulverized glass and plaster; the joints of the second were luted with a putty made of sesquioxide of iron and linseed oil, and over this the cement of glass and lime was spread. The fire-pots were lined with brick. Every precaution was used to render the joints gas-tight.

The coal used was anthracite; the two varieties, " red " and " white ash," being mixed together in equal parts. The experiments conclusively proved that at no time were carbonic acid and carbonic oxide absent from the library heated by the furnaces. During the days when a breeze was blowing outside, causing a brisk draught, the amount of these gases present was very small; but in dull, moderate weather, the increase was quite perceptible: carbonic oxide appeared to predominate, and it was proved that, in the imperfect combustion which takes place in furnaces, this dangerous agent is largely in excess of all other products. Sulphurous acid was present whenever a new supply of fuel was added to the fire, and usually when any interference was had with the furnaces. The shaking of the contents of the fire-pot by means of the grate-handles invariably caused the ascent into the room of much fine dust and ashes, mingled with the air current. This impalpable dust is not usually noticed by the occupants of rooms where furnaces are used. It is only when, through very imperfect and leaky joints, large amounts of ashes, and even cinders, are allowed to escape, that many families complain. It is astonishing how negligent or indifferent most housekeepers are to the presence of agents destructive to comfort and health. We have been informed by a very extensive manufacturer and dealer in house-warming apparatus, that in one hundred furnaces which came under his observation for repairs, more than three-fourths had the air chambers and passages obstructed by coal ashes. It was no unusual circumstance to remove a bushel from some chambers through which the heated air passed to the rooms of the dwellings. What an unhealthy, deleterious mixture of air and ashes must here be produced for children and adults to breathe! From investigation, we believe there are but few furnaces in use in this country which do not allow of the escape of ashes into the air flues; and a more intolerable nuisance we are unacquainted with, unless it be the deleterious gases which usually accompany the dust in the air current. The injury to furniture, books, curtains, paintings, etc., from this dust-impregnated air is very great. In portable furnaces, besides the bad joints connected with the interior parts, the outside coverings and doors fit very imperfectly, and much dust finds its way into the air passages from the cellar or basement in which the furnace is placed.

The results of the experiments undertaken prove that the gaseous products of combustion do pass through cast-iron under certain conditions. Some portions of the cast-iron work of furnaces are more readily permeable to gases than others. In many cases, the fire-pot is surmounted by a high dome, cast in one piece. This forms the heat-radiating portion. In casting this, the metal is turned into the mould so as to bring the rim, or edge, fitting to the fire-pot, uppermost; consequently, the crystalline structure is different, or less dense, at that portion nearest the fire, and under the favorable influences of greater heat and less density this part of the dome affords the easiest egress for the gases.

It is impossible to construct furnaces or stoves of cast-iron, and secure impermeability to gases.

They should not be made in part of cast-iron and in part of wrought-iron; as it is proved that wherever the two come together, there oxidation goes on with great energy. In the summer months, when furnaces are not in use, the ashes deposited about the joints become moist, and wherever thin iron pipes are connected with cast-iron shoulders, there the work of oxidation goes on, and the whole is soon destroyed. This energetic action is due to galvanic currents, resulting from the different crystalline structure of the metals.

After patient practical trial of two of the best and most popular forms of furnaces, it was apparent that inventors and manufacturers had not yet supplied apparatus which was not open to serious, or even fatal, objections; certainly no one that we had examined could be permitted to remain in operation in our dwelling for even the briefest space of time.

The objections or defects may be stated to be: *first*, the employment of *cast-iron* in the interior construction; *second*, the presence of joints in the air chamber, which cannot be made perfectly tight by lutes or cements; *third*, arranging the air chambers or flues so that ashes and dust can pass into the air current; *fourth*, the imperfect arrangement of smoke flues and dampers, by which great loss is incurred from incomplete combustion; *fifth*, needless complication, and consequently needless expense in construction.

FARM PENCILLINGS AT LAKESIDE.

AS we sit in the shade of the trees on the shore of the beautiful Kenoza at Lakeside, we take our pencil and put upon paper the thoughts upon nature, rural life, agriculture, horticulture, etc., which naturally come to us while thus at rest and alone. We are not quite alone, however, for we have the pleasant company of the birds and squirrels that flutter and chirp about us. How beautiful is this scene upon this glorious June morning! The lake shimmers and sparkles in the light, as the sun climbs the opposite hills and pours its slanting rays through the rich foliage upon the peaceful waters. The sky is of the deepest blue, and the earth is carpeted with the intensest green. Wild flowers are scattered in profusion everywhere; the buttercups and the dandelions, with their tints of yellow blending with the green, give to the landscape a richness of coloring which no painter can imitate. The drops of dew, not yet dissipated by the warmth of the sun, rest upon the grass and the shrubs, and glisten like the purest gems. The transparent waters of the lake afford to the eye a clear look into its depths, and its pebbly bottom is seen far away from the shore where we are sitting, and we can watch the movements of the perch and pickerel foraging for their morning meal. The earth is in its holiday attire; the waters, just escaped from the icy bonds of winter, are joyous as an infant when it awakes from the sweetest slumber; the air is laden with the odors of flowers and the songs of birds. Rest, rest, peaceful rest — of this let us have our fill. Let us forget the city, its noise and dust, and the bargainings and wranglings of restless men; let us commune with Nature, study her lessons, observe her laws, and thus be made wiser, happier, better. A friend from the city the other day, lounging by our side under the trees, asked if we did not think that those who were permitted to enjoy much of rural life would have some deductions made from the happiness of the life beyond. This was a random thought presented in jest, and prompted doubtless by the satiety of enjoyment which those only feel who emerge for the first time from winter life in the city. Such excursionists into the country have rather exaggerated notions of the inequality with which enjoyment is distributed among men, and their estimate of the pleasures of rural life is based upon the brief hour they pass under the trees. The difference in amount of absolute enjoyment in this world is very much less than is supposed. Every man regards his neighbor as having at his command sources of happiness denied to himself. The poor man envies the stately mansion, the horses and carriages, and the luxurious table of the rich. The rich man would give all his possessions to buy the health, the sweet slumber, and the freedom from care that his poorer neighbor enjoys; and so we recognize the wisdom of Providence in establishing the immutable law by which happiness is meted out in about equal measure to all who seek it with pure motives.

Happiness depends much upon the sensibilities, and very much upon how we educate ourselves. We may live in the midst of the most beautiful manifestations of nature, and through insensibility or sordidness be incompetent to enjoy them. It is true, also, that in order to enjoy city or country life it is necessary that we experience some of the toils, inconveniences, and vexations of both, and be able to escape from the one or the other at will. By contrast with the brick walls and the hurly-burly of the city, the country seems a paradise; but for those tied to the country, and compelled to toil in the fields, the city possesses extraordinary attractions. From our present point of view rural life appears beautiful, and the language of poetry is quite inadequate to describe the peacefulness and delights of the scene. *We* are under the trees, with the glorious lake before, and the farm behind us. Over yonder, in the meadow, is Mike, a genuine Hibernian, in a straw hat and a striped shirt, with sleeves rolled above the elbows, showing brawny arms which, under the influence of sun and air, have acquired a hue like that of hemlock-tanned leather. He has milked his tenth cow this morning, and driven the herd to the hill pasture, where they are now busily at work nipping the white clover blossoms fresh with dew. We have sent him to the meadow to pull up by the roots some burdock plants, the seeds of which during the winter washed in from the highway. Mike declares this to be "sweaty work," and "terrible for the back." From the experiment of extracting a half dozen of the long-rooted plants, we conclude he is more than half right.

Let us "interview" Mike, and learn his opinion regarding rural life, farm work, etc. "Well, Mike, this is a fine morning; what a happy fellow you must be, out here in the green meadows, with the birds making music for you, and the winds filling you so full of sweet scents as even to mask the odor of that old pipe, the stem of which has found its way out through a hole in your pocket. Tell us, Mike, what you think of these beautiful scenes, and farming matters in general." "Indade, sir, the mornin' is a fine one, to be sure, but I haven't heard any birds; and as to the air, it is good enough, what there is of it, but if there was more of it 'twould cool me off a bit; and as to the scents, they don't trouble me. Farming, sir, is hard work, airly and late, dig, dig, all the time; what with the cows, and the milkin', and the weeds to pull, and corn to hoe, there is small time to take a whiff from the ould pipe. Fine gintlemen, that can lie on the grass all day, don't know what farming work is, beggin' your pardon, sir, for bein' so plain with you."

And Mike's plainness is excusable. He don't hear the birds sing, nor smell the sweet odors of flowers. A plug of tobacco has a more grateful fragrance to him than buttercups or violets; and as to the air, it is only fine, when there is enough of it to cool his sweaty brow. A visit to the city, after haying, is an event to which he looks forward as the one great thing in the future. But after all, Mike is happy; he has but few wants, and fewer cares. If his back aches at night, from using the hoe, or swinging the scythe, it is "all right" in the morning after six hours of sound slumber. Although insensible to the beautiful things in nature, he finds compensation for this in the harmony with which the physical mechanism works, and in the robust health enjoyed, and in the narrowness of the world in which he moves, which affords no scope for ambition, and gives rise to but few artificial wants.

WINTER LIFE OF PLANTS.

The cool winds and the hoar frosts of the autumn months have aided in the sad work of stripping the trees, shrubs, and grasses of their rich summer attire, and they are now for the most part standing cheerless and bare. Here and there a late-blooming flower may be seen, or a narrow patch of green grass in some warm, sheltered nook, on the margin of the lake; but the great and active operations of Nature in building up and sustaining vegetable structures have ceased, and soon a snowy mantle will be cast over field and wood, and the deep sleep of winter will commence. The corn, wheat, and other grains, with the roots and grasses, have been safely housed; and the farm-work of the summer is ended. The herds seek shelter in barns, the squirrels in trees, and the birds take flight to a sunnier clime. We must imitate their example, and flee from our lake-shore retreat to the library or parlor, where the genial heat from the blazing wood in the open fire-place dispels all feelings of sadness or discomfort, and puts us in a mood even to welcome the reign of snow and ice. As we look out upon the bare fields this morning, we are led to pencil down some thoughts upon the *winter life of plants*. It is an error to suppose that in winter, in our climate, there is a dead calm in plant life, and that Nature is wholly palsied in her movements. Wherever the rays of sunlight fall, there is never perfect rest; and this relates to the vegetable as well as to the animal world. Sunlight is pregnant with life; no matter how slant may be the rays, or how few the hours during the twenty-four they may fall upon the earth. In winter the really useful plants cannot grow, but in the lower forms of cryptogamic plants the processes of vegetation are quite active. The mosses, lichens, liverworts, etc., resist cold wonderfully, and they will grow at very low temperatures. We find them under snow-banks and sheets of ice in winter keeping up an active circulation, so active that they are able to ripen their sporangia or mature their fruit, with the thermometer close upon zero. Lichens are so constituted as to be able to reverse the order of nature, and take their winter nap in summer. In the cold months their vegetating period occurs, and they are then most active. The lichens are a very low order of plants; but we must not look upon them with contempt, for from their existence, or by their creation, life upon our planet is rendered possible. The poor, humble lichens came before man; and man would never have come at all, if the lichens had not preceded him. These plants are the very first which made their appearance upon the rocks, when our earth was barren and chaotic; and dying there, they prepared the way for a higher vegetation. At the present time there are few rocks so barren or smooth that the tenacious lichens will not fasten upon them and flourish through storm and cold, as do the cereals in the best of soils and in the warmest sunshine. Suppose the reader becomes interested in these statements, and starts out botanizing some day in the coming winter months. Such an excursion will by no means be devoid of interest or instruction. Everywhere on rocks, fences, and fallen trees, and in the pebbly bottoms of brooks, the rich mosses will be found in great variety; and their study will open up new ideas of the wonderful nature of plant structures, even in their lowest forms.

But activity in plant life in winter is not alone confined to the cryptogamia. It is during this inclement season that many of our forest trees ripen and perfect their seeds. The firs and pines are not like the deciduous trees, which allow the moisture they contain to freeze in winter. The temperature of a pine-tree under the bark never falls below the congealing point, no matter how severe the cold may be outside. These resinous trees keep up a kind of low "tree heat," as do the bears a low animal heat, in freezing weather. Consequently the circulation of sap goes on, and the immature seeds are ripened. In some localities in the northern part of our country those evergreens grow which bear true leaves, like the ivy, laurel, or perhaps the holly. We call these plants evergreens; but in fact they change their leaves as do the deciduous varieties. The change is made gradually, one leaf dropping off when another has grown to replace it, and so the tree is never wholly deprived of its foliage. It is probable that in winter there is considerable vegetative activity in these evergreens, as it is impossible that these changes can take place when the sap is completely dormant. Sunlight and warmth are agents of tremendous power in connection with plant activities. If in the depth of winter a mild day occurs, we shall find, by making incisions in the stem or branches of trees, that the slumbering forces are partially awakened, and the sap is in motion.

If we allow that in the higher orders of flowering plants winter is a time of repose, it can hardly be supposed that there is no interchange of matter between the air and the body of the plant, for some such movement is needful to its life. The hibernating animals in their dens are practically dead, but still a feeble form of life remains; the heart slowly beats, and waste goes on. There is, in fact, a continuous interchange of particles between the air and the body, and so there must be between the air and all plant structures. Men and animals sleep during the night-time, but the functions of life go on undisturbed. Winter to deciduous trees and herbaceous plants is their night-time, when they sleep, to recuperate their vital energies, and become prepared for the labors of reproduction when the spring opens. As is the case with human beings, it is better that this sleep be continuous and undisturbed, in order that full strength may be had for work in the season of activity. A winter in which there are many fitful changes, first warm and then cold, is unfavorable for the growth and perfection of seeds and fruit; and trees and plants suffer more from these causes than from drought or wet in summer.

We have spoken of the trees as being bare of foliage in winter; but this is not absolutely true, for trees have winter leaves as well as summer leaves. The winter leaves are less apparent, but they are no less real or perfect. If we take from a tree one of its buds, and examine it carefully, we shall see that it is composed of a little bunch of true leaves, nicely compressed together in layers, resembling fish-scales. These are the winter leaves of trees, and every species has them perfectly characteristic of its kind.

This winter dress of trees is no apparel suddenly formed, or put on late in the autumn; it is the growth of all the spring and summer months. During the hot season, when the sap is active, it was diverted away from the buds by the great demands of the expanding summer foliage, so that their growth was slow. They remain immature until the summer leaves begin to fall, when the sap flows towards the buds, and they are perfected. The winter dress of trees has a purpose in the economy of plant life. The structure in winter does not demand nutrition, but it must have protection, and this the buds afford. In them is stored up all the beauty and glory of the vegetation of the coming year, and thus they possess an interest of the highest kind. Nature is very careful of these buds, for it seems to be understood that in them exist latent forms of life, most intimately connected with the welfare of the race. In order fully to protect them, they are compressed together very tightly in the smallest possible space, and are covered in under an air-tight and water-tight roof. The outer layer of buds is either covered by a warm coat of fine hairs, or cemented closely with a resinous or glutinous secretion, which resists the action of water. How wise and careful is Nature in all her wonderful operations! Can we doubt for a moment the existence of a great and good Being, who guides and directs all these movements?

REMINISCENCES OF AN EXPERIMENTER.

IN examining recently the contents of certain dark attics and closets in some of our buildings, we came upon confused heaps of wheels, magnets, coils, batteries, retorts, alembics, beakers, pyrometers, galvanometers, etc., etc., encumbering the shelves and floor; many of which were curious enough in the rudeness of their form and construction, and aptly illustrative of the science of a former period.

In these piles of rubbish, the cast-off *débris* of many years of study and toil, is written the history of the progress of discovery for more than three decades. Here is an electro-magnet, with lever-attached armature, and an arrangement of wheels, — the remains of rude telegraphic apparatus which we had in operation in 1845, about the time Morse's experiment began to attract attention; here are iron cups, connected with copper and platinum conductors, designed to illustrate the practicability of exploding magazines under water by electricity; here are galvanic batteries of every conceivable form and size, most of which are now cast aside as practically useless; and also discs and cylinders, of glass and rubber and gutta-percha, for experiments in statical electricity; here is a formidable iron cylinder, which resembles a piece of ordnance, designed for the purpose of solidifying, or rather liquefying, carbonic acid gas, — a fashionable experiment twenty years ago. In overturning the dusty contents of the rooms we discover apparatus illustrative of the discoveries and inventions of each decade. At the commencement of the last, we have the *spectroscope*. This instrument is probably the first one ever constructed and used in this country. It was made for us by the late Mr. Fitz, of New York, in 1860, immediately upon the appearance of Bunsen's and Kirchhoff's papers upon spectrum analysis.

A third of a century devoted to the study of the physical sciences, and their practical, experimental investigation, is an interesting period to look back upon. How greatly extended have been the boundaries of human knowledge, how vast and sublime the results of scientific labor and research! How many important and useful discoveries and inventions have had their birth and development in that period! We have lived to see a thousand timid, hesitating suggestions in science ripen into demonstrated facts; to see a thousand important truths snatched from the domain of surmise, conjecture, or doubt, and transferred to that of established, unquestioned certainty.

A third of a century ago, when our labors began, we had no lines of telegraph, no ocean steamships, no street rail-cars, no photographic pictures, no aniline colors, no kerosene oil, no steam fire-engines, no painless surgical operations, no gun-cotton, no nitro-glycerine, no aluminium, no magnesium, no electro-plating, no spectroscope, no positive knowledge of the physical constitution of the stellar worlds, and but five hundred miles of *slow* steam railway in the United States. Our telescopes and microscopes were defective, and comparatively of low power, and we had few of those delicate scientific instruments now so important in every department of research.

The last third of a century has been the most active, the most important period of time that has elapsed since time began. Indeed, more of the great resources of Nature have been developed, more of her intricacies unravelled, a deeper penetration made into her mysteries, than in all the six thousand years since the advent of man upon our earth.

Do we who have lived during the accomplishment of these results, and perhaps actively participated in them, realize the stupendous greatness of this epoch? It is difficult to do this. We are pleased to talk about it, but our natures do not admit of a full realization of the importance of modern scientific discovery. We are whirled past these great events as our planet is whirled through the interplanetary spaces; we know it moves with tremendous velocity, but its motions are wholly unobserved.

The reminiscences of an experimenter and student in science for a period of a third of a century are always of the deepest interest, but they are not always of the most pleasing character. There are recollections of so many instances of the rankest injustice done to ingenious, toiling, self-sacrificing fellow-experimenters, which have sprung from jealousy, selfishness, or hate, that the desire is sometimes felt that the powers of memory might be abridged at will. Many of the books in which great discoveries are described and claimed have the wrong names upon the title-page. So powerful is the influence of *prestige* and great names, most of these errors, we fear, will never be corrected.

There are also recollections of disappointments and sad failures in the results of experiments; often some great truth or principle has apparently been within easy grasp, when, lo! unexpected hindrances or errors were discovered, and all our exalted imaginings and dreams of a name immortal vanished into thin air, and from a flight most lofty we were compelled to gravitate down to earth again.

Experimental labor is exacting, expensive, and in some departments perilous. It is exacting, because it demands the whole time and the most intense thought. The hours of the day when other kinds of labor are prosecuted, and which cease with the setting sun, do not suffice for the experimenter. An idea or difficult scientific problem, pressing on the mind, becomes almost a material object there; and if it were a brick, or a lump of lead, it could not more effectually disorder the natural functions of the brain and prevent sleep. A great deal of agitation is made over the hours of labor at the present time, and eight hours of labor and sixteen of rest are clamored for by an influential party. This relates to physical labor. Hard work in this world is not alone the lot of those who handle the hoe and spade, or swing the sledge-hammer. The laborer in the field of experimental research reverses the modern idea, and devotes sixteen hours to work, and eight to imperfect rest.

Experimental research is expensive, as there is a constant drain upon the purse for the implements wherewith to prosecute the labor. Platinum and gold and silver, among the expensive metals, are requisite, and in a thousand little ways money disappears as if by magic. From imperfect memoranda in our possession it is shown that we have expended, during the past third of a century, for apparatus and materials, more than *sixty thousand dollars*. This does not relate, of course, to the large working apparatus in our manufacturing establishment, but solely to that needed in experimental labor. Most of this is now thrown aside as worthless, or retained only as interesting relics of the past.

The experimenter in some departments, as in that of chemical manipulation, is constantly liable to accidents which endanger life and limb. We can look back upon a score of explosions and narrow escapes from vapors and poisonous gases, and the indelible scars remaining show how painful have been some of these casualties. But, upon the whole, the retrospective glances of an experimenter are of the most interesting and pleasant character; and no youth who has the necessary qualifications, the intelligence, the ingenuity, the perseverance, the enthusiasm, should be deterred from entering this field because of the exhausting, exacting, or expensive nature of the labors.

When we review in this way the experiments of bygone years, several inventions and art processes, regarded as very new and wonderful by the multitude, seem quite old to us. We have watched the progress and adventures of these art processes and devices for many years with the same interest that parents watch the career of their children, for the reason that they are indeed the children of our brain. Many of our readers have doubtless noticed the huge piles of what is called "leather board," heaped upon the sidewalks and in the leather stores of our cities. Seventeen years ago we made the first sheet of the article ever produced in the United States, or in the world. Noticing the immense heaps of " leather scraps" (the worthless refuse of shoe factories), which are seen in New England towns, we conceived the idea, in 1854, of attempting to utilize them by disintegrating, or tearing them into fine shreds, and forming from the particles a cheap leather board which might serve many useful purposes in the mechanic arts. An old paper-mill, belonging to the late Mr. Flagg, of Exeter, New Hampshire, was hired for the purpose of experiment, and after surmounting many difficulties, we succeeded, during the year, in manufacturing several tons of the new article. As soon as the problem was fairly worked out, it was allowed to pass into the hands of other parties, who have since carried on the manufacture upon an immense scale. No patent protection was sought, and no remuneration for our labors has ever been received. An exclusive right to make this article, on a patent protection, would have been worth a great many thousand dollars. Although the production of the "patent leather," as it is often called, has been of advantage to producers, its invention has not been particularly advantageous to the consumers of shoes. The interior "soles" of most cheap shoes are now constructed of this material, and when water penetrates into them, the result shows that it is a poor substitute for good leather. We fear that *paterfamilias* will never thank us for devising "leather board."

Twenty-three years ago, we engaged in a series of extended experimental investigations upon the hydrocarbon liquids, and one of the results of these labors was the production of an apparatus for lighting buildings by employing air for the conveyance of the light vapors to gas burners. From this invention have come all the "portable gas machines," "gasoline apparatuses," "air lights," "automatic gas" devices, which are so numerous in our cities. Every one of these is claimed as "very *new*," and all are covered by "patents." The perusal of an article published in the "Traveller" newspaper of Boston in 1849, describing the results of our labors, will show that but few important improvements have been made in our original devices, during more than twenty years. Sixteen years ago we constructed an apparatus for extinguishing fires by the employment of carbonic acid, or aerated water under pressure. The instrument was almost precisely similar to the one now claimed as *new*, and

owned by a company who control the *right* to make
"Fire Annihilators." We did not at the time we
invented the apparatus, nor do we now, regard it as
of much practical importance. Nearly seventeen
years ago we put in position the first apparatus for
cooling mineral waters and syrups at the place of
outlet, or upon the counter of the dealer. All the
new "soda water" devices seen in the shops are
based on our original device, and are but modifica-
tions of our invention. Upon this no patent protection was secured, but we have been informed by
an extensive manufacturer that its value at present
would be not less than *fifty thousand dollars*. The
numerous devices which have been lately introduced
for protecting lamps and fluid cans from explosions
are simply the reappearance of contrivances which
we made public twenty or more years ago. At
that time we covered metallic lamps with glass, and
prevented flame from entering the reservoir by a
chamber of wire gauze; and also some wick ar-
rangements, now claimed as new, are found in our
old lamps. Time is worse than wasted in en-
deavors to make lamps *safe* which are designed to
hold and burn dangerous, inflammable liquids.
More severe accidents are caused by spilling and
igniting the liquids than by explosions. The inflammable light naphthas sold so often as kerosene,
cannot be harbored in any dwelling with safety.

No matter what lamps or cans are used, the danger is not in any important degree removed by their agency. There is safety only in expelling everything of the kind from household use.

We might increase the list of so-called "new inventions," which originated with us many years since, but our object is not to " tell what we have done," but to present some reliable examples, illustrating the nature of many of the "new patents" which are constantly thrust upon public attention. Our readers may have reason to thank us for affording them some insight into the merits of the claims of those who seek from them pecuniary assistance.

INFECTIOUS GERMS.

THE spread of the new cattle disease, *epizoötic aphtha*, in this country, under circumstances so remarkable, has awakened in the minds of farmers and others a desire to learn something of the nature of the contagious principle, and the mysterious manner in which it is communicated from one animal to another.

An agent of infection so subtle that a dog or cat walking through a barn where diseased animals are kept, and then running four or five miles in the open air and entering another barn, infects a herd of healthy animals without contact, must be regarded as extraordinary in its nature. After all, it is no more extraordinary or wonderful than the infectious germs of small-pox, scarlet fever, or measles, which are readily conveyed very long distances in the clothing, and in the air, and which remain uninfluenced by meteorological agencies, heat and cold, wet and dry. The susceptibility of different individuals to the influence of contagious germs is no less wonderful than the nature of the germs themselves. It may be said that no two persons are affected alike by them, and it is probable that the same difference prevails among animals. Indeed, we have instances of some herds attacked by the new disease, in which five, ten, and even twenty per cent. of the animals remain in perfect health. They are confined in the same stalls with those diseased, and breathe the poisoned air night and day, and yet not a function is disturbed or a vital movement interfered with. Among human beings, we know that a physician, nurse, or any person leaving a room in which there is a patient sick with scarlet fever or measles, may, in passing a child upon the opposite side of the way, communicate to it the disease; while during the same walk another may be taken in the arms and suffer no detriment. There is a small class of persons who can never be brought under the influence of kine-pox virus, and such are usually greatly distressed in consequence of this idiosyncrasy of organization. There is but little occasion for anxiety, however, for such will usually escape the more severe disease of small-pox, if exposed to infection. In our view, those who are most readily and severely influenced by vaccine virus are the persons who will be most likely to contract varioloid, when brought in contact with the germs of small-pox; so that the feeling of safety cherished by such is not well founded. There are individuals and families in every community who are continually suffering from every form of malaria, poison, and contagion known to medical men, and certainly they are deserving of sympathy. Personal cleanliness and the strict observance of all hygienic laws are of no avail with thousands in warding off these disturbing agencies; they are the victims of an organization susceptible to the malign influences of poisons and contagions which lurk constantly in the atmosphere, and even in food and drinks.

We know but little regarding the exact nature of the germs which are capable of implanting disease in the system. That they have substance and form, no one can doubt. As distinct atoms or particles of matter, they are inconceivably small, and capable of being buoyed up or supported in air, and carried from place to place through its agency. In a barn containing animals suffering from pleuro-pneumonia, or from the epizoötic aphtha, we must suppose the atmosphere to be loaded with the infinitesimal particles. If our eyes could be opened so that we could see the particles as we see snowflakes in the winter, what a fearful spectacle would be presented! The disgusting, poisonous atoms would be seen flying in all directions, and resting upon everything; upon the clothing of those in charge of the animals, upon the hay, upon the manure, floors, scaffolds, and upon the backs of any dogs, cats, or birds which might be present. A perfect shower of infectious spores would be seen to prevail, and probably we should no longer wonder how the poison is carried so rapidly from one point to another. It is probable that when one or more of these germs are taken into the system through the organs of respiration, a kind of fermentation is set up in the blood, analogous, perhaps, to that which occurs in vegetable substances during the vinous or acetic change.

In studying disease, or any of the changes which occur in the animal organization, we must constantly bear in mind that the body is simply a piece of chemical apparatus, and that all the movements or changes that occur are simply chemical reactions of one form or another. The disease germs themselves are chemical substances; and the difference in chemical composition gives rise to the different forms of blood poison which manifest themselves as scarlet fever, measles, typhus, etc., in human kind, and pleuro-pneumonia, hoof and mouth disease, etc., in animals.

There is reason to suppose that scarlet fever, measles, and typhus ferments resemble albumen in complexity, and like albumen they may be altered in composition and action by heat, alcohol, and other agents. Small-pox ferment is of a different kind, and is remarkable for the small quantity of substance which produces such extraordinary changes. An atom so small that a microscope of the highest power is incapable of defining it, enters the system through the lungs, and passes on into the blood, and from thence into every texture, nerve, and secretion. In a few days the chemical actions of oxidation and nutrition throughout the whole body are completely altered, and the little particle of matter has reproduced itself infinitely. Pustules appear over the whole skin surface, each one loaded with an infinite number of germs identical in nature with the original particle which set in motion the train of disorganizing forces. There is general peroxidation going on; there is inflammation of the ears, the eyes, the mucous membranes, the joints, the serous membranes; everywhere there is great chemical disturbance. This is *small-pox*, and the terribly disgusting, wretched condition of the bodily functions is due to the introduction of a particle so infinitesimally small that no optical instrument can discern, and no balance can weigh it.

The poisonous germs producing intermittent fever, or *fever and ague*, from whatever source they may arise, are probably of a highly complex and nitrogenous nature, and are capable of being dried and carried great distances by the wind. They enter by the mouth with the dust, pass into the blood, and soon produce a kind of fermentation, which results in high fever preceded by a chill. After this is over, the poison is spent in part; but during the remission of from one to three days, sufficient is reproduced to go through the same action again. This remarkable poison, producing intermittent chill and fever, will work on, unless utterly destroyed by medication, until the victim is so far weakened as to falter and die. The ague ferment is totally unlike that producing small-pox and measles, for by the action of the latter the textures of the body are so changed that they are incapable of going through the same process again; but one can have ague a dozen or more times in the course of his life. It is indeed a great mercy that some of our worst zymotic or infectious diseases can attack us but *once*.

We might as well expect to learn the nature of soul or spirit, as to expect to obtain any precise knowledge of the chemical differences in the germ poisons which affect men and animals. How can we ever know anything regarding the actual difference between a germ producing pleuro-pneumonia or disorganization of the lungs in a cow or ox, and one producing suppurating sores and ugly ulcers in the mouths and hoofs of the animals? Both are specific poisons, exerting specific action upon different parts of the animal organization. It is inconceivable how this can occur; and yet perhaps it is no more inconceivable or mysterious than most diseases, which, after all, are but derangements of the chemical reactions or forces of the animal economy.

We can manage and control chemical changes quite perfectly when they occur in inorganic bodies, and, thanks to science, we can manage tolerably well those which occur in the human or animal organization when they happen under ordinary conditions, and are not of too violent a nature. There is a class of reagents called "remedies," which, when rightly used, serve to control in some degree destructive chemical action in the body. We have learned that the poisonous germs which we have had under consideration cannot maintain their vitality in the presence of certain chemical agents, among which are carbolic and cresylic acids, sulphurous acid, the chlorides of some of the metals, etc. These destroy the life of spores, as arsenic or prussic acid destroys life in the human body, and therefore they are the proper agents to employ to arrest the spread of infectious diseases. By using proper caution, by observing the laws of hygiene, by keeping the body clean, and the blood in good condition, by plenty of air and exercise, we can in a considerable degree fortify ourselves against the attacks of poisonous germinal affections.

THE FOOD OF PLANTS.

THE most delightful and instructive of the studies connected with the farm relate to plant life, and the food of plants. It may seem to many that a consideration of the food of plants implies the necessity of a belief in the possession by plants of certain organs or powers of digestion and assimilation, and this belief should be entertained, for it is founded upon fact. Plants do indeed in a most proper sense eat and drink, and they are as capricious in regard to the kind and quality of the food which they demand as are animals or human beings. It is as interesting to study the nature of the appetite and wants of a stalk of corn, or wheat, or a blade of timothy, as that of a child which the mother so carefully and anxiously watches and tends during the weeks and months of early infancy.

What a mystery there is in the life of a plant! How does a tree, or a shrub, or a blade of grass, grow? This interrogatory has often been put to men of science, and the patient researches which have been made, by the aid of that beautiful and wonderful instrument, the modern microscope, enable them to give a tolerably satisfactory answer. The nature of the substances employed in building up the plant structure is well understood, and also the form of mechanism which is adopted in the first beginnings of growth, and the chemical changes and transformations which occur; but the nature of the *vital force* which guides, and upon which all activity depends, we do not understand, and it is probable that human research will never shed much light upon this mysterious but most interesting problem. The little microscopic cell is the workshop in which great changes are elaborated, and during the season of vegetable growth this is the seat of the most intense activity. Every plant that grows upon our earth, however great or small, must be considered as having originated from a single cell, so infinitesimally minute, that the highest powers of the microscope are required to observe it. If we turn over one of the pebbles common in our brooks, we shall find a slimy material of a greenish hue, adhering to its under side. This covering is a true plant, but it is one of the lowest of known forms. If we examine it with the microscope, it will be found to be perfect in structure, having an organism so wonderful as to command our admiration. Feeble and insignificant as it is, it corresponds in structure with the huge oak which grows by the stream and overshadows it with its branches. The plant that adheres to the rock consists of a single cell, but that cell is as perfect and beautiful as any of those which make up the structure of the oak. The tree is but an aggregation of cells; cells piled upon cells, and the work that is carried on within them is no more complex than that which goes on in the workshop of the humble unicellular plant.

It is with a choice of terms that we designate the cell as the workshop of the plant, in which the materials that enter into its organization are elaborated and fitted to aid in the increase of its substance. The nature of the food which is manipulated within the cell is indeed peculiar, inasmuch as plants gather together the waste products of men and animals, and again fit them for the use of higher organisms. Plant food is oxidized food — food which it is impossible for animals to assimilate; and the plant, in all its functions and in the objects of its growth, manifestly occupies an intermediate position between ourselves and the insensible rocks. This is absolutely essential to the existence of man upon the earth. Of all the functions of plants, the most remarkable are connected with, or related to the solar rays, for they possess the power of utilizing the sun's heat in a way which enables them to pull apart, as it were, some of the most complex and refractory compounds known to modern chemistry. The most tiny, feeble leaf, or blade of grass, has a power in chemical decomposition greater by far than is possessed by Liebig, Boussingault, or any of the great experimenters of the age. The separating in silence, in the quiet of the meadows, by organisms so frail that we can crush them between the thumb and finger, of a compound so fixed as carbonic acid, is one of the marvels in nature which puzzles and confounds the philosopher, and leads him to bow in humility before the God of nature, whose power so infinitely surpasses that of man. But after all, this analytical power of the plant is no less amazing than its synthetical capabilities. The work of tearing apart oxidized bodies, is immediately followed by that of rearranging the elements, and forming new compounds still more complex, and into these, as a fixed principle, less oxygen is allowed to enter. The great work of the plant is, to disassociate oxygen from compounds, and thus store up energies which are made apparent when we burn vegetable substances as fuel upon our hearthstones, or as food in our bodies. All the forces resulting from heat and muscular exertion have their origin in plants, and however great may be the exhibition of power, the leaves of the trees, and the grasses of the field, have utilized or elaborated it all from the solar rays.

Although the food of plants, as well as the

method of appropriating it, differs from that of animals, there are analogies not only apparent but real between them. In animals we have the respiratory functions, and so we have in plants, for plants breathe as truly as we do ourselves; we require our food to be composed of certain elements arranged in certain combinations, — so do plants; we find it essential that our food should be in particular forms or mechanical conditions, — so do plants; we must be regularly supplied with food, and this is the case with plants. These are some of the similarities existing between plants and animals, and serve to show how intimate is the relation which subsists between plants and the higher forms of organized structures.

Although we have learned with certainty regarding the elements essential to plants, and also the forms of combination required, we have yet to learn the exact mode in which they acquire their food, and how they are able to build up such bodies as cellulose, starch, albumen, oil, etc., from these elements. No processes which chemists venture upon in the laboratory are found so difficult as the synthetical production of organic compounds. Indeed, organic chemistry has thus far proved totally incompetent to instruct how to form any one of these bodies from the elements, and for their elaboration we must look solely to the vital chemistry of animals and plants.

THE FOOD OF PLANTS. 267

It is a well understood fact that without plants, animals could not exist upon our planet. In the wonderful economy of things it is absolutely essential that there should be some intermediate or connecting link between ourselves and the mineral kingdom, and plants constitute this important link in the chain of life. The three kingdoms, animal, vegetable, and mineral, are correlated, and involved in a cycle of changes, which are unintermitting, and wonderful in their nature. We are incapable of being nourished by any form of mineral substances, but such nourish plants, and are transformed by them into vegetable tissues and products; and subsisting as we do upon plants, we draw support indirectly from the insensible rocks. The plant consumes the rock dust, and attracts to itself the carbon of air and earth; we transform these into flesh and bones, and, as a last step in this perpetual circulation of matter, after death they relapse again into their dead inorganic condition.

It was formerly thought by chemists that plants lived upon humus, a compound entirely organic in its nature, and when some of the metals were found in the ash of plants, they were regarded as accidental ingredients, or extraneous bodies which somehow intruded themselves into the incinerated mass. In our time, we know that these mineral bodies enter the vegetable structure as food, and that it cannot exist without them. The mineral portion of plants is small indeed, compared with the nitrogenized and carbonaceous parts, and this paucity of the mineral substances was undoubtedly the reason why the early experimenters were led into error.

At present, we are acquainted with sixty-five elements or primary bodies, of which all things animate and inanimate are made. Twenty-two of these have been found in plants, and therefore are to be regarded as food material. Let us for a moment consider the strange metals and other substances which plants absorb into their structures. Among the metals we find iron, potassium, calcium, sodium, magnesium, manganese, copper, cæsium, rubidium, and zinc. It has been stated that arsenic has been found in plants, but this is doubtful. The non-metals are iodine, bromine, fluorine, chlorine, phosphorus, silicon, carbon, hydrogen, nitrogen, oxygen, and sulphur. Nothing can appear more singular than the fact that the refractory metal, iron, can find its way into the stalks and leaves of plants, or that the rarer metals should be hunted out of the soil by them, and appropriated as food. Some varieties of plants have peculiar appetites, and require most extraordinary elements in order to thrive. Tobacco is one of these, and the ash which clings to the end of the smoker's cigar con tains substances found in but one or two other plants known to man. Among the rarer bodies are the newly discovered metals cæsium and rubidium, and how or where the plant obtains them is indeed a mystery, as the most delicate chemical tests have failed to detect these elements in soils. In common garden beets, also, the same substances have been found. Copper has frequently been observed in vegetable products used for food, and what is very singular, the metal has recently been discovered in the feathers of birds, and some of the tints in the plumage are due to its presence. The fluorine which is found in the enamel of teeth, in men and animals, comes from plants, as does also the manganese which accompanies iron in the blood. Aluminium, the metal which within a few years has been regarded with special interest, as of great service in the arts, has been found in certain species of Lycopodium, and zinc has been found in the *Viola caliminaria*, a plant common in some sections of France. Bromine and iodine are found in the marine *algæ*, or sea weeds, and for a long time the entire amount of these important substances employed in medicine and the arts was derived from sea plants cast on shore by the waves.

The organic constituents of plants, elaborated or formed from combinations of the elements, carbon, hydrogen, nitrogen, and oxygen, make up the largest portion of their bulk, and therefore must be regarded as of essential importance as food. Before considering the sources and value of these agents to vegetable structures, it will be interesting to examine briefly the conditions under which plants start into existence, and the forces or agents which are involved in developing and sustaining the embryo before the plant has the power of seeking its own food.

In all the changes and evolutions constantly going forward in the vegetable world, the sunbeam plays a most important part. Analysis of a sunbeam shows that it possesses three distinct functions or powers. It is capable of supplying light and heat, and also it has *actinic* force, or the capability of producing chemical decomposition and recomposition. Upon the chemical influence of the sun's rays depends the germination of seeds, as well as the growth of the plant. We bury the seed in the ground and shut it out from the influence of light, but we do not place it beyond the reach of the sun's actinic influence, for that penetrates like heat to the little earthy couch where the embryo plant lies hid, and arouses it into life. Light, or the luminous rays of the sun, so important to the well being of the plant, is actually inimical to the excitation of vitality in the seed. How singular is this fact! A series of carefully conducted experiments have proved that seeds will not germinate in light, although supplied with heat and moisture, when the actinic rays are cut off. Deprived of the luminous rays, with the actinic in full force, they spring into life with great rapidity. Seeds sown upon the surface of the earth will scarcely germinate, as soil cultivators very well know; and on the other hand, seeds buried deep, so that the actinic rays cannot reach them, will certainly perish. The planting of seeds so as to secure the proper distance below the surface is a most important point in husbandry, as it has much to do with the early starting of the plants, and the success of the crops.

How beautiful and wonderful is the process of germination, when the chemical and vital phenomena are set in motion by the actinic rays! The starchy particles of the seed become converted into gum and sugar upon which the young plant feeds. The tiny root peeps out from the husk, and with mysteriously directed powers plunges downward into the fertile soil. The slender plumule pushes upward towards the light. The soil cracks and heaves, and the infant vegetable emerges fresh and moist into the world of air and sunshine, with the unfolding of the first pair of leaves; and with the first lighting of the sunbeam upon their tender tissues commences a series of chemico-vital phenomena wholly different from that of the preceding stage of existence. The plant is now fairly dependent for food upon its own energies, and root and leaf are the theatres of great activities.

None of the elements named as constituting the food of plants exist as such in them, save oxygen and nitrogen. Half the weight of a dried plant is carbon, and yet it does not exist in it as free carbon; it is all locked up in combinations of greater or less complexity. There is not one of these elements of food that can be supplied to the plant in its naked condition, as they not only have no power to nourish, but are positively poisonous. There is much misapprehension regarding these points among farmers, which arises from not clearly understanding the statements of writers upon the chemistry of agriculture. Not unfrequently inquiries are received concerning the cost of nitrogen, carbon, phosphorus, etc., and sometimes orders are sent for these agents, which are designed to be used for fertilizing purposes. While it is true that nitrogen is an element needful in the nutrition of plants, it must be presented not alone, but in one of two forms of combination,—either as ammonia, or nitric acid; and further, the acid must be in association with an alkali, as soda or potash, in order to be safely employed by the farmer. In either one of these forms, it is of immense value as plant food. Nitrogen is a gaseous

THE FOOD OF PLANTS. 273

body, and has neither taste, color, nor smell. It cannot be burned, it will not support combustion, and it cannot be breathed into the lungs. It is a strange, negative element, and yet without its influence not a stalk of corn nor a blade of wheat can grow. It is the most costly of all our fertilizing agents, and yet millions and billions of tons are present in the air constantly, and every plant is surrounded by and immersed in it. Is not this statement perplexing or paradoxical? Nitrogen as it exists in nitrogenous bodies is alone available for plants, and the cheapest source, outside of refuse animal compounds, is in the form of nitrate of soda. This salt, known as Chilian saltpetre, is sold at the present time at about four cents per pound, which makes the nitrogen it contains cost about twenty-eight cents per pound. The nitrogen in sulphate of ammonia, at present market rates, costs thirty-five cents, and I have not found it so readily available, or prompt in its action upon my fields. For grass lands, as a top dressing, the nitrate of soda has proved with me a profitable agent. It brings in the better quality of grasses, and largely increases the crops. It should be pulverized fine, mixed with an equal quantity of fine seasoned peat, and sown evenly over the field, giving to each acre two or three hundred pounds of the salt. Without a supply of nitrogenous food plants become feeble and ultimately die; and hence we must supply it in some form, either as it exists in manure, or in commercial substances. The soil does not furnish it in sufficient abundance, neither does the atmosphere, in any available form. There is always a little ammonia in moist air, which comes from decaying animal or vegetable matter, and also there are traces of nitric and nitrous acids in rain water, but these sources of supply are wholly inadequate to the wants of plants upon most fields.

An acre of wheat yielding twenty-five bushels requires, in straw and grain, forty-five pounds of ammonia. The results of careful experiments show that under the most favorable circumstances no more than ten pounds of ammonia is ever supplied to an acre of soil by rain-water; so if all the ammonia of the rain-fall is assimilated, thirty-five pounds in addition would have to be supplied, to meet the wants of the wheat field.

Carbon, the agent so largely consumed by plants, fortunately costs us nothing. The farmer need not trouble himself concerning this important element in plant food, for the atmosphere furnishes an abundant supply for all our wants. It is supplied in the form of carbonic acid, and we do not know that it can be assimilated through any other carbon compound. A carbonate, unless it be of potash or soda, is practically valueless to the farmer.

Carbonate of lime, in any form, cannot be regarded as a fertilizing substance having a commercial value. Very strenuous attempts have been made to induce farmers to purchase ground clam and oyster shells, the venders alleging that they were equal to ground bones in fertilizing value; but this is a fraud of a serious nature. Clam shells are composed of carbonate of lime, while bones are made up of the phosphate of lime, — quite a different substance, chemically and agriculturally considered. The shells are composed of carbonic acid and lime, the bones of phosphoric acid and lime, the former acid having no money value, the latter having a high value.

Calcic carbonates should not be confounded with sulphate of lime, which is plaster or gypsum. In this substance sulphuric acid, or oil of vitriol, is in combination with the lime, in place of carbonic acid, and a very different chemical and fertilizing agent is supplied. It has high value as an application to some fields, although its action is not well understood. The experiments which the writer has made with plaster go to prove that its good effects are due rather to the acid than the lime. It has the power of fixing the ammonia of the atmosphere, and forming sulphate of ammonia, which is a salt of much value. In applying gypsum to soils, it must be remembered that but a small quantity can be made available in a season, as it requires nearly five hundred pounds of water to bring one pound of it into solution. Half a ton is a sufficient dressing for an acre of ground.

The element hydrogen is freely supplied to plants by dew, mist, and rain, and therefore is costless to the husbandman. It is only through water that hydrogen can be presented to the plant, but this is by no means its only important office. It enters the plant as water, and it is through its agency that all the various forms of food are rendered assimilable. It is the liquid medium which holds all the inorganic substances, and from the aqueous current which unceasingly flows through the little cells of plants, they are absorbed and appropriated as food.

Enormous quantities of water annually descend upon the land. If the rain-fall be but twenty inches per annum, it corresponds to something like two thousand and twenty tons of water falling upon each acre every year. Much of this is carried off by evaporation, or through drainage. Still, a large proportion is retained by growing plants, or passes through them, aiding in most important functions. It can be shown that a gallon of water passes through a single plant of wheat in a season, and the aqueous exhalations from the broad disc of a common sunflower each day amount to six or eight ounces.

THE FOOD OF PLANTS.

The wonderful substance (formerly so rare and costly), phosphorus, is so essential an ingredient in the food of plants, that not one of any kind can flourish without it. This highly combustible body, so offensive to taste and smell, and withal so poisonous, enters the plant in combination with oxygen, with which it forms phosphoric acid. The entire supply of phosphorus employed in the arts comes from plants, and they hunt it from the soil atom by atom, and incorporate it into their structures. Animals feeding upon plants abstract the element, and it takes its place in the bones in combination with lime, forming basic phosphate of lime. We gather the bones of the dead animals, and after calcination, subject them to chemical treatment, and thus isolate the phosphorus in a pure state in large quantities. How curious is this cycle of changes and transformations! We can in no way obtain a clearer conception of them, than by reflecting upon the fact that the phosphorus found upon the end of every friction match we use in our dwellings has been gathered from the soil by vegetables, and passing through their organization, it has taken its place in the bones of oxen, cows, or horses, and from thence passed into the laboratory of the chemist, where it is fitted to subserve the most useful purposes. If this substance had a tongue, what an interesting history of adventures it could unfold!

The amount of phosphorus or phosphoric acid in the soil is usually insufficient to meet the wants of the plant, and hence the farmer must furnish supplies if he wishes to increase his crops. Formerly there were but two sources of supply, that from manure or animal excrement, and that from the bones of animals; but now we have a third source in the mineral coprolites, or phosphatic deposits, found upon the coast of South Carolina. From these substances what are popularly known as superphosphates are made and sold largely in the market.

Potash holds a most important place in the list of substances consumed by plants, and hitherto much anxiety has been manifested regarding a supply equal to our wants. A few years ago we were acquainted with no sources of the agent save that of the ash of plants, and as mineral coal came into use for furnishing household warmth, wood ashes and the potash salts obtained from them became very scarce and costly. Every year the farmer removed from the soil large quantities of potash in his crops, which he could not return again through the excrement of his animals, and therefore it was evident his lands were becoming impoverished to an alarming extent. High cultivation, as respects potash, increases this impoverishment, as all cultivated plants are richer in this substance than those growing spontaneously. To obtain a clear understanding of the needs of the soil, it may be stated that an acre of wheat producing 25 bushels of grain, and 3,000 pounds of straw, removes about 40 pounds of potash in the crop. Can any farmer conceive of that amount of potash existing in the soil of any one acre of land upon his farm? We know it must be present, and within easy reach of the plants, else not a blade of wheat can grow and mature the seed. Nearly all soils of course contain potash, but the quantity is often insufficient for crops of any of the cereal grains. A crop of corn, of 100 bushels to the acre, removes in kernel and stalk 150 pounds of potash and 80 pounds of phosphoric acid. We cannot raise large crops of corn without furnishing potash in some assimilable form, for a small crop of fifty bushels to the acre requires about 75 pounds of the agent. A fair crop of oats, say 50 bushels to the acre, removes only about 13 pounds of potash. Barley and rye remove not far from 30 pounds each.

Now we have observed the great deterioration in our potato crops during the past ten or twenty years, and what is the cause of this alarming decrease of tubers? Can science, can chemistry point out the reason, or aid in remedying the difficulty? I think it can, and in order to understand the matter it is necessary to understand the kind and amount of food which the potato demands. A field of potatoes yielding 300 bushels to the acre will remove *from* the soil in tubers and tops at least 400 pounds of potash; also it will remove 150 pounds of phosphoric acid. Now these amounts are very large, and show that the potato plant is a great consumer of the two substances, and also show that in order to restore our potato fields to their former productive condition, we must supply phosphatic compounds and substances holding potash in large quantities. For six or eight generations in New England our fathers have been exhausting the soil, by removing these agents in their potato and other crops, and we have reached a time when the vegetable is starving in our fields for want of its proper food. Our farmers have found that new land gives the best crops, and this is due to the fact that such fields afford the most potash. But so long as we crop our pastures so unreasonably, we cannot resort to new land, as land is not *new* that has had its potash and phosphatic elements removed by grazing animals. A potato field which gives but 100 bushels to the acre requires at least 140 pounds of potash, but by allowing the tops to decay upon the field, 60 pounds are restored to the soil again, as that amount is contained in them. A medium crop of potatoes requires twice as much phosphoric acid as a medium crop of wheat, so that in two years with wheat the land is deprived of no more of the agent than it loses in one year with potatoes.

The aim has been in this essay to point out the nature of the materials which plants require, and to impress upon the mind of the reader the great truth that when the farmer has gained this knowledge, and also learned the quantity necessary for a given crop, the accumulation and use of these materials are as simple as supplying raw materials for making cloth, boots and shoes, or any other manufacture. A field in proper condition for culture should contain in ample abundance all the inorganic materials which the intended crop requires, and these materials should be in an assimilable condition, or in other words, they should be in a soluble condition, so that by the aid of water they can be taken up and carried through the plant organism. The proper manures for wheat and corn are the nitrogenized varieties, or those which hold nitrogen, either in the form of ammonia or as nitric acid. These should be conjoined with phosphates and potash in considerable amounts. For potatoes, potash, phosphates, and lime are required; the latter element, lime, enters largely into the leaves, and is an important article of food for the vegetable. Gypsum or plaster, which holds lime and sulphurous acid, is a valuable manurial agent for potatoes, especially on moist land. But enough has been said to show that each variety of plants demands peculiar kinds of food, and unless this is supplied by the soil, or through our agency, it is impossible for them to flourish.

There has never been a time when soil cultivation, as a pursuit, was more hopeful or promising than the present. We have just learned the important fact that an abundance of plant food has been stored up for our use in mines and rocks, and that we have only to reach out our hands and take all that we require. Ten years ago who could have dreamed even of such vast deposits of potash as have been opened up to us at the Stassfurth salt mines in Germany. Some idea of the supply may be formed from the fact that at the present time more potash is furnished from these mines than from the wood-ash sources of supply of the whole world. Only about 13,000 tons of potash were sent to market from the United States and British America in 1870, and yet from Stassfurth, where a dozen years ago it was not supposed that a single ton could be procured, 30,000 tons of the muriate of potash were manufactured and supplied to consumers upon both continents, during the past year. The surface salts at these mines, which hold the potash, are practically inexhaustible, and millions of tons will be supplied in succeeding years. No doubt our own salt mines will be found upon careful examination to afford potash, and hence we may look with confidence to the rapid cheapening of this most useful product.

Ten years ago who could have supposed that along the river beds upon the coast of South Carolina there were millions of tons of rocks holding that important element of plant food, phosphoric acid? These rocks were indeed known, but their important character was not understood. The phosphatic rock beds of that region extend over an area of several hundred square miles, and in some places they are twelve feet thick. It is estimated that from five hundred to a thousand tons underlie each acre. How vast is this supply of an agent of the highest importance to agriculture, and what a source of national wealth it opens to us!

Two important considerations force themselves upon our attention. One is, that nature has provided ample materials to supply all our wants. In mountains, and caverns, and streams, she has deposited all elements and combinations which are essential for our well-being and progress, and it is unreasonable and wicked to doubt regarding the future. The other is, that science must be sustained and fostered, for it holds the key which is alone capable of unlocking nature's storehouses, and bringing forth from the dark recesses of earth those rich materials which have been provided for our sustentation and happiness.

www.ingramcontent.com/pod-product-compliance
Lightning Source LLC
Chambersburg PA
CBHW031333230426
43670CB00006B/337